TURKISH SHORT STORIES FOR BEGINNERS

20 Captivating Short Stories to Learn Turkish & Grow Your Vocabulary the Fun Way!

Easy Turkish Stories

www.LingoMastery.com

CONTENTS

INTRODUCTiON

So you want to learn Turkish? That's awesome!

Like any other foreign language, it's going to open the doors to discovering a completely new culture. Whether you're learning Turkish for work, studies or fun, the knowledge of the language will broaden your mind, let you meet new people, and will become a new page in the thrilling book of your self-development.

Heard about Turkish being impossibly hard to learn? That might be true. But that's what we're here for. Rely on this book that was written with your needs in mind and accept the challenge without any fear or doubts.

What is the following book about?

We've written this book to cover an important issue that seems to affect every new learner of the Turkish tongue — a lack of helpful reading material. While in English you may encounter tons (or gigabytes, in our modern terms) of easy and accessible learning material, in Turkish you will usually and promptly be given tough literature to read by your teachers, and you will soon find yourself consulting your dictionary more than you'd want to. Eventually, you'll find yourself bored and uninterested in continuing, and your initially positive outlook may soon turn sour.

Our goal with this book will be to supply you with useful, entertaining, helpful and challenging material that will not only allow you to learn the language but also help you pass the time and make the experience less formal and more fun — like any particular

1

lesson should be. We will not bore you with grammatical notes, spelling or structure: the book has been well-written and revised to ensure that it covers those aspects without having to explain them in unnecessarily complicated rules like textbooks do.

If you've ever learned a new language through conversational methods, teachers will typically just ask you to practice speaking. Here, we'll teach you writing and reading Turkish with stories. You'll learn both how to read it *and* write it with the additional tools we'll give you at the end of each story.

The stories are for Beginners. What does it mean?

We don't want the word to be misleading for you. When thinking about you as a beginner, we focused on combining two things:

1) provide you with easy to understand words and structures;
2) avoid simplistic content.

Judging by our extensive experience, it's impossible to make any impressive progress by dealing with the material that you are absolutely comfortable with. Dive into the unknown, make an effort, and you'll be rewarded.

To make things easier for you, we picked only common words – no rocket science, that's for sure. You won't encounter any complex sentences with multiple clauses and prepositions.

Just take the last step — apply your diligence and work hard to go over to the next level.

The suggested steps of working with the book

1. First, just read the story. Chances are you already know many words.

2. Then read it again, referring to the vocabulary. Note that our vocabulary is much easier to use than a conventional dictionary because:

   a) the words are listed in order of their appearance in the text;
   b) the translations are given in the very form you find them in the text;
   c) the most complex words are given as word combinations to let you grasp the grammatical structure.

3. Now that you think you understand the major plot of the story, check yourself by referring to the summary of the story that is provided both in Turkish and English.
4. Go over to the Questions section to check if you've understood the details.
5. Check if you were right in the Answers section.
6. And at last — time to enjoy. Read the story once again, getting pleasure from the feeling of great achievement. You deserved it!

What if I don't understand everything?

Remember — understanding each and every word is not your goal. Your goal is to grasp the essence of the story and enrich your vocabulary. It is **absolutely normal** that you may not understand some words or structures and that sometimes you may ultimately not entirely understand what the story is about. We're here to *help* you in any way we can.

If you don't know some word and it's not in bold (i.e., not in the vocabulary list), then

   – You may have already encountered it but in a different form. Challenge your attention!

- The word may be of an international character. What could the word 'такси' – [taksi] mean? Right! It's 'taxi'.
- Use the context. Let's turn to the 'taxi' example again. What can you possibly do with a taxi? Right, you can call or catch it!

Other recommendations for readers of *Turkish Short Stories for Beginners*

Before we allow you to begin reading, we have a quick list of some other recommendations, tips and tricks for getting the best out of this book.

1. Read the stories without any pressure: feel free to return to parts you didn't understand and take breaks when necessary. This is like any fantasy, romance or sci-fi book you'd pick up, except with different goals.

2. Feel free to use any external material to make your experience more complete: while we've provided you with plenty of data to help you learn, you may feel obliged to look at textbooks or search for more helpful texts on the internet — do not think twice about doing so! We even recommend it.

3. Find other people to learn with: while learning can be fun on your own, it definitely helps to have friends or family joining you on the tough journey of learning a new language. Find a like-minded person to accompany you in this experience, and you may soon find yourself competing to see who can learn the most!

4. Try writing your own stories once you're done: all of the material in this book is made for you to learn not only how to read, but how to write as well. Liked what you read? Try writing your own story now, and see what people think about it!

FREE BOOK!

Free Book Reveals The 6 Step Blueprint That Took Students
From Language Learners To Fluent In 3 Months

One last thing before we start. If you haven't already, head over to
LingoMastery.com/hacks and grab a copy of our free Lingo Hacks
book that will teach you the important secrets that you need to
know to become fluent in a language as fast as possible. Again, you
can find the free book over at LingoMastery.com/hacks.

Now, without further ado, enjoy these
20 Turkish Stories for Beginners.

Good luck, reader!

Chapter I

BÜYÜKANNEMİN NESİ VAR? —
WHAT'S WRONG WİTH MY GRANDMA?

Beş yaşındaydım. **Büyükanneme** neler olduğunu **anlamıyordum.** **İlaçlarını** nereye koyduğunu, **faturaları** ne zaman **ödeyeceğini,** markete **nasıl gideceğini** unutuyordu. **Oysa** daha önce hiç **böyle** değildi. **Her zaman** çok **düzenli** bir **insandı.** Bizim **unuttuğumuz** şeyleri bile o **hatırlar,** bize söylerdi.

— Büyükannemin **nesi var?** **Eskiden** çok düzenli ve **planlı** bir insandı. **Şimdi** her şeyi **unutuyor,** yoksa **hasta** mı? diye **sordum** anneme.

— Büyükannen **yaşlanıyor,** diye **yanıtladı.**

— Yaşlanmak **nasıl bir şey?** Her yaşlanan insan **unutkan** mı olur? Ben de mi öyle **olacağım?** dedim.

— Yaşlanan **herkes** unutkan olmaz **canım.** Büyükannende Alzheimer **hastalığı** var. **Bu** hastalık **insanların** unutkan olmasına **yol açan** bir hastalık, dedi annem.

Annem çalışıyordu. Bu yüzden evde büyükanneme bakacak kimse yoktu. Annem ve babam, büyükannemin evde tek başına yaşamasının tehlikeli olabileceğini düşünüyorlardı. Bu yüzden onu bakımevine götürmeye karar verdiler. Böylece her ihtiyacı olduğunda birinden yardım alabilecekti. Biz de onu sık sık ziyaret edecektik.

Üzülüyordum çünkü büyükannem artık **bizimle** yaşamayacaktı. **Evini** özleyecekti. Ben de **onu** çok özleyecektim.

— Orada **yeni arkadaşları** olacak, dedi annem.

— Onu istediğimiz zaman **ziyaret** edebilir miyiz? diye sordum.

— Tabii ki. **Hafta sonları** onu görmeye gideriz. **Hediyeler** de götürürüz, dedi.

— **Dondurma** götürebiliriz. **Çilekli** dondurma. Büyükannem çileğe **bayılır**, dedim heyecanla.

— Tamam, çilekli dondurma **götürebiliriz**.

Büyükannemi ziyaret ettiğimizde **hüzünlendim**. **Neredeyse** ağlayacaktım. Büyükannem **koltukta** üzgün bir şekilde **oturuyor**, dışarıdaki **ağaçlara** bakıyordu. Çok **güçsüz** ve **yalnız** görünüyordu. Yanına gidip ona **sarıldım**.

— **Bak** büyükanne, sana **hediye** getirdik. Çilekli dondurma, senin **en sevdiğin**, diyerek dondurma kutusunu **ona verdim**.

Büyükannem **hiçbir şey** söylemedi. **Kutuyu** açtı ve dondurmayı yemeye başladı.

— Bak, çok **sevdi**, diye rahatlatmaya çalıştı beni annem.

Ama ben **hayal kırıklığı**na uğramıştım:

— Sanki bizi tanımadı, dedim.

— Ona biraz **zaman** vermelisin. **Daha sık** ziyaret ederiz ve buna **alışır**, diye yanıt verdi annem.

Fakat büyükannemi **bir sonraki** ziyaretimizde de her şey **aynıydı**. Büyükannem dondurmayı **yedi**, bize **gülümsedi** ama hiçbir şey söylemedi.

— Büyükanne, beni gördüğüne **sevinmedin mi**? diye sordum.

— **Sevindim** çünkü sen bana dondurma **getiriyorsun**, dedi büyükannem.

— Büyükanne, benim **kim** olduğumu **biliyor musun**?

Büyükannem gülümsedi ve **yüzüme** baktı:

— Sen dondurma getiren **kız**sın.

— Evet ama ben senin **torun**unum. Beni hatırlamıyor musun? dedim ve **kollarımı** onun **boynuna** doladım.

Büyükannem yeniden gülümsedi.

— **Hatırlamak** mı? Tabii ki hatırlıyorum. Sen dondurma getiren kızsın, dedi.

O an, büyükannemin beni **bir daha** hiç hatırlamayacağını anladım. **Yanlızlıklarla dolu** ve **kendisine ait** bir **dünyada** belirsiz **anılarla** yaşıyordu.

— Seni çok seviyorum büyükanne, dedim.

O sırada büyükannem ağlamaya **başladı**.

— **Sevgi**... Seni çok sevdiğimi **hatırlıyorum**. **Niçin** seviyordum seni? Bunu hatırlayamıyorum. **B**elki de dondurma getirdiğin için. Neyse..., **Boş ver**... Seni seviyorum ve bu **çok güzel**.

Bunun üzerine annem:

— **İşte bak** canım, onun **tüm istediği** bu. Sevgi! dedi.

— O zaman **her gün** ona dondurma getirelim. Beni **hatırlamasa bile** ona sarılacağım, diye cevap verdim.

Çünkü sevgiyi hatırlamak, **birinin ismini** hatırlamaktan daha **önemli**ydi.

Hikayenin Özeti

Bu hikaye, anlatıcının büyükannesi ile olan çocukluk anılarından birini anlatıyor. Büyükannesi yaşadıklarını ve etrafındaki insanları unutmaya başlamıştır. Çocuk bu durumun nedenini anlayamayacak kadar küçüktür. Bu durumu annesine sorduğunda büyükannesinin çok yaşlandığını ve Alzheimer hastası olduğunu öğrenir.

Aile, büyükanneyi bakımevine götürmeye karar verir çünkü evde onunla ilgilenecek kimse yoktur. Onu sık sık ziyaret ederler. Bu ziyaretlerden birinde küçük çocuk, büyükannesinin artık onu hatırlamadığını fark eder. Fakat büyükannenin hatırladığı bir şey vardır: Sevgi.

Summary of the story

This story tells one of the narrator's childhood memories about her grandma. Her grandmother has begun to forget her experiences and people around her. The kid is too young to understand the cause of this situation. When she asks her mother about the situation, she finds out that her grandmother is very old and suffering from a disease, Alzheimer.

The family decides to take the grandma to the nursing home as there is no one at home to care of her. They go to visit her often. During one of these visits, the little girl notices that her grandma no longer remembers her. However, there is something her grandma still remembers: Love.

Vocabulary

- **beş:** five
- **büyükanneme:** my grandma (dative)
- **anlamıyordum:** I didn't understand
- **ilaçlarını:** her medicines (accusative)
- **faturaları:** the bills (accusative)
- **ödeyeceğini:** that she will pay (accusative)
- **nasıl gideceğini:** how you/he/she will go (accusative)
- **oysa:** but, in fact
- **böyle:** so
- **her zaman:** everytime, whenever, always
- **düzenli:** neat
- **insandı:** person (past tense) [She was such a ... person]
- **unuttuğumuz:** that we forget
- **hatırlar:** remembers
- **nesi var:** what's wrong with him/her/it
- **eskiden:** once, before
- **planlı:** organized
- **şimdi:** now
- **unutuyor:** she forgets
- **hasta:** sick
- **sordum:** I asked
- **yaşlanıyor:** she is getting old
- **yanıtladı:** she replied
- **nasıl bir şey:** what is it like
- **unutkan:** forgetful
- **olacağım:** I will be
- **herkes:** everyone
- **canım:** my dear
- **hastalığı:** 's disease (possessive)
- **bu:** this
- **insanlar:** people
- **yol açan:** that causes
- **annem:** my mom
- **bu yüzden:** so
- **kimse:** no one
- **tek başına:** on her own
- **tehlikeli:** dangerous
- **düşünüyorlardı:** they thought
- **bakımevine:** to a nursery home (dative)
- **böylece:** thus, in this way

- **ihtiyacı:** her need
- **yardım:** help
- **sık sık:** frequently
- **üzülüyordum:** I was feeling sorry
- **bizimle:** with us
- **evini:** her home (accusative)
- **özleyecekti:** she would miss
- **onu:** her (accusative)
- **yeni:** new
- **arkadaşları:** her friends
- **ziyaret:** visit
- **hafta sonları:** weekends
- **görmeye:** to see
- **hediyeler:** presents
- **dondurma:** ice cream
- **çilekli:** strawberry [ice-cream]
- **bayılır:** she likes so much
- **götürebiliriz:** we can bring
- **hüzünlendim:** I felt sad
- **neredeyse:** almost
- **koltukta:** on the chair (locative)
- **oturuyor:** sitting
- **ağaçlara:** trees (dative)
- **güçsüz:** weak
- **yanlız:** lonely
- **sarıldım:** I hugged
- **bak:** look
- **hediye:** gift
- **en sevdiğin:** your favorite
- **ona verdim:** I gave her
- **hiçbir şey:** nothing
- **kutuyu:** the box (accusative)
- **sevdi:** she liked
- **hayal kırıklığı:** disappointment
- **zaman:** time
- **daha sık:** more often
- **alışır:** she gets used to
- **bir sonraki:** next
- **aynıydı:** was the same
- **yedi:** she ate
- **gülümsedi:** she smiled
- **sevinmedin mi:** aren't you happy
- **sevindim:** I am happy
- **getiriyorsun:** you are bringing
- **kim:** who
- **biliyor musun:** do you know
- **yüzüme:** at my face (dative)
- **kız:** girl
- **torun:** grandchild
- **kollarımı:** my arms (accusative)

- **boynuna:** her neck (dative)
- **hatırlamak:** to remember (infinitive)
- **an:** that moment
- **bir daha:** anymore
- **yanlızlıklarla dolu:** full of loneliness
- **kendisine ait:** on her own/belonging to her
- **dünyada:** in world (locative)
- **anılarla:** with memories
- **başladı:** she started
- **sevgi:** love
- **niçin:** why
- **belki:** maybe
- **boş ver:** never mind (imperative)
- **çok güzel:** very good, very beautiful
- **hatırlıyorum:** I remember
- **bunun üzerine:** then
- **işte bak:** see
- **tüm istediği:** all she wants
- **her gün:** everyday
- **hatırlamasa bile:** even though she doesn't remember
- **çünkü:** because
- **birinin ismini:** someone's name (accusative)
- **önemli:** important

Questions about the story

1. **Çocuk annesine "Büyükannemin nesi var?" diye sorduğunda ne oldu?**

   a) Annesi ona kızdı.
   b) Büyükannesinin yaşlandığını söyledi.
   c) Babasına sormasını söyledi.
   d) Soruyu duymazlıktan geldi.

2. **Ailesi, büyükanneyi … götürmeye karar verdi.**

   a) Dondurmacıya.
   b) Mezarlığa.
   c) Ona aldıkları yeni eve.
   d) Bakımevine.

3. **Onu ziyaret etmeye gittiklerinde büyükanne neyi izliyordu?**

   a) Televizyonu.
   b) Futbol oynayan çocukları.
   c) Ağaçları.
   d) Bakımevindeki yeni arkadaşlarını.

4. **Çocuk, büyükannesini ziyaret ettiğinde ne fark ediyor?**

   a) Büyükanne torununu hatırlamıyordur.
   b) Büyükanne artık çilek sevmiyordur.
   c) Annesi ile babası boşanmak üzeredir.
   d) Büyükanne, bakımevinde kalmaktan çok memnundur.

5. **Büyükanne, çocuğu neden sevdiğini hatırlamaz. Doğru mu, yanlış mı?**

   a) Doğru.
   b) Yanlış.

Answers

1) B – She told her that her grandma is getting old.
2) D – To the nursery home.
3) C – Trees.
4) A – The grandma doesn't remember her grandchild.
5) A – True.

Chapter II

KASIM SABAHI — NOVEMBER MORNİNG

Soğuk bir kasım **sabah**ıydı. Jack **yataktan** kalktı, gideceği **toplantı** için **hazırlanmaya** başladı. İstanbul'a **dün** gelmişti. Çalıştığı **şirket**, Türk **ortaklar**ıyla yapacağı **toplantı** için onu **göndermişti**. Jack, Türkçe **biliyordu**. **Dil** öğrenmeye **meraklıydı** ve bildiği **pek çok** dilden **birisi** de Türkçeydi.

Saat 08.00'de otel **odasından** ayrıldı. Hava çok soğuktu. **Kahvaltı** yapmak ve **ısınmak** için ufak bir **kafeye** girdi.

— **Çay** var mı? diye sordu **garsona**.
— **Elbette**, efendim.

Kahvaltı bittiğinde saat **çoktan** 9 olmuştu. Masadan **aceleyle** kalktı ve **toplantıya** gitmek üzere **yürümeye** başladı. Toplantının yapılacağı yer **uzak** değildi. Bu yüzden **taksiye** binmesine **gerek yoktu**.

Birkaç **dakika** sonra çok **şiddetli** bir **ses** duydu. **Siren** sesi... Ne olduğunu anlayamadı. **Nereden** geliyordu bu ses? **Acil** bir durum mu vardı? **Ne** yapması gerekiyordu?

Jack çok şaşırmıştı. Fakat şaşkınlığının **asıl** sebebi bu sesler değildi. **Etrafındaki** her şey **bir anda donmuştu**. Onunla beraber **sokakta** yürüyen **insanlar**, **arabalar**... Her şey olduğu yerde **hareketsiz** şekilde **duruyordu**. Tüm **şehir** bir anda **heykeller** ile dolmuştu sanki.

"**Ne oluyor**? Neden kimse **hareket etmiyor**?" diye düşündü.

Birkaç **saniye** sonra siren sesleri durdu. Arabalar yine **hareket etmeye**, insanlar **yeniden** yürümeye başladılar. **Hâlâ** çok şaşkındı.

Sonunda toplantının yapılacağı **binaya vardı**. Türk ortakları olan şirketin **sekreter**i onu **bekliyordu**.

— **Hoş geldiniz**. **Yolculuğunuz** nasıl geçti? Burayı **kolay** bulabildiniz mi? diye sordu sekreter **kız**.

— **Merhaba**. Evet, **kaldığım otel** buraya çok **yakın**. Fakat gelirken çok **tuhaf** bir şey **oldu**. Bir anda siren sesleri çaldı ve her şey **durdu**, diye yanıt verdi Jack.

Sekreter ona gülümsedi:

— **Bugün** 10 Kasım.

— Anlamadım, dedi Jack.

— 10 **Kasım**, Türkiye'nin **kurucu**su olan Atatürk'ün **vefatının yıl dönümü**dür. Bu tarihte saat 09.05'te, **ülkenin her yerinde** siren sesleri duyulur.

— Ah! Peki, **neden** 09.05?

— Atatürk **tam** o saatte vefat etmiştir.

— **Şimdi** anladım.

— Evet. Her 10 Kasım'da saat dokuzu beş **geçe**, **ülkede** her şey durur. İnsanlar bir dakika **boyunca** onu **anmak** için **yaptıkları her şeyi bırakırlar** ve **saygı duruşu**na geçerler. Bu süre boyunca Atatürk'ün **bizim için** neler yaptığını ve ona ne kadar çok şey **borçlu** olduğumuzu düşünürüz.

— Bunu **bilmiyordum**. Acil bir durum olduğunu **sandım**. Filmlerdeki **uzaylı istilaları** ya da **doğal afet**ler geldi **aklıma**. Herkesi birden **etkileyen** nasıl bir şey olmuş olabilir, diye düşündüm.

Sekreter gülmeye başladı.

— Bunu **tarihinizdeki** başka **liderler** için de yapıyor musunuz? diye sordu Jack.

— Hayır. **Yalnızca** Atatürk için.

— **O zaman** Atatürk çok **büyük** bir **adam** olmalı.

— Atatürk bu **ulus**un atasıdır. Bugün **özgür** insanlar olarak yaşıyorsak bunu Atatürk'e **borçluyuz**. Onu, çok seviyor ve **her zaman hatırlıyoruz**.

— Atatürk ne kadar **şanslı** bir lidermiş, dedi Jack.

— Şanslı olan **biziz,** diye cevap verdi sekreter kız.

İşi bittiğinde oteline dönerken **bir an önce** odasına çıkmak ve **bilgisayarını** açmak için sabırsızlanıyordu. Bu **olağanüstü** insan, yani Atatürk hakkında **daha fazla bilgi** almak için kısa bir **araştırma** yapmalıydı.

Hikayenin Özeti

Jack iş toplantısı için İstanbul'a gelmiştir. Toplantıya giderken aniden siren sesi duyar. Çok şaşırır çünkü sokaktaki herkes hareket etmeyi bir anda bırakmıştır. Jack ne olduğunu anlamaya çalışırken her şey yeniden hareket etmeye başlar. Siren sesleri durmuştur.

Toplantı yerine vardığında onu sekreter karşılar. Jack ona yolda olanları anlatır. Sekreter ona o günün, yani 10 Kasım'ın Türkiye'nin kurucusu olan Atatürk'ün vefatının yıl dönümü olduğunu açıklar. Siren seslerinin sebebi budur. Türk halkı, büyük liderlerine olan saygısını, onun için bir dakikalık saygı duruşuyla göstermektedir. Jack bu durumdan çok etkilenir ve Atatürk hakkında daha fazla şey öğrenmek ister.

Summary of the story

Jack comes to Istanbul for a business meeting. On his way to the meeting, he suddenly hears a siren. He gets shocked because everything on the street has suddenly stopped moving. As Jack tries to figure out what is going on, everything starts moving again. The sirens have stopped.

When he arrives at the meeting place, the secretary welcomes him. Jack tells her everything that happened on his way to the meeting. The secretary explains to him that that day, 10th of November, is the anniversary of the passing away of the founder of Turkey. That is the reason of the sirens. The Turkish people show their respect to their great leader with one minute of silence for him. Jack has been really impressed and wants to learn more about Atatürk.

Vocabulary

- **soğuk:** cold
- **sabah:** morning
- **yataktan:** bed (ablative)
- **toplantı:** meeting
- **hazırlanmaya:** getting ready (dative)
- **dün:** yesterday
- **şirket:** company
- **ortaklar:** partners
- **toplantı için:** for the meeting
- **göndermişti:** it has sent
- **biliyordu:** he knew
- **dil:** language
- **meraklıydı:** he was interested in
- **pek çok:** many
- **birisi:** one of (possessive)
- **saat 08.00'de:** at 8 o'clock
- **odasından:** his room (ablative)
- **ayrıldı:** he left
- **kahvaltı:** breakfast
- **ısınmak:** to warm (infinitive)
- **kafeye:** to cafe (dative)
- **çay:** tea
- **garsona:** to waiter (dative)
- **elbette:** of course
- **çoktan:** already
- **aceleyle:** in a hurry
- **toplantıya:** to the meeting (dative)
- **yürümeye:** walking (dative)
- **uzak:** far
- **taksiye:** taxi (dative)
- **gerek yoktu:** there was no need
- **dakika:** minute
- **şiddetli:** loud
- **ses:** sound
- **siren:** siren
- **nereden:** from where (ablative)
- **acil:** emergency
- **ne:** what
- **asıl:** real, main
- **etrafındaki:** around him
- **bir anda:** at once
- **donmuştu:** it was frozen
- **sokakta:** on the street (locative)
- **insanlar:** people
- **arabalar:** cars
- **hareketsiz:** still, motionless

- **duruyordu:** he/she/it was standing
- **şehir:** city
- **heykeller:** statues
- **ne oluyor:** what's going on
- **hareket etmiyor:** it's not moving
- **saniye:** second
- **hareket etmeye:** moving (dative)
- **yeniden:** again
- **hâlâ:** still
- **sonunda:** at last
- **binaya:** to the building (dative)
- **vardı:** he arrived
- **sekreter:** secretary
- **bekliyordu:** she was waiting
- **hoş geldiniz:** welcome (interjection, formal/plural)
- **yolculuğunuz:** your trip (plural/formal)
- **kolay:** easy
- **kız:** girl
- **merhaba:** hello
- **kaldığım otel:** the hotel where I stay
- **yakın:** close, near
- **tuhaf:** strange
- **oldu:** it happened
- **durdu:** it stopped
- **bugün:** today
- **Kasım:** November
- **kurucu:** founder
- **vefatının:** of passing away (possessive)
- **yıl dönümü:** anniversary
- **ülkenin her yerinde:** all over the country (locative)
- **neden:** why
- **tam:** sharp [09.05 sharp], exact
- **şimdi:** now
- **geçe:** past [half past nine]
- **ülkede:** in the country (locative)
- **boyunca:** for (minute), throughout, during
- **anmak:** to commemorate (infinitive)
- **yaptıkları her şeyi:** everything they are doing (accusative)
- **bırakırlar:** they stop
- **saygı duruşu:** moment of silence
- **bizim için:** for us
- **borçlu:** owed
- **bilmiyordum:** I didn't know
- **sandım:** I thought

- **uzaylı istilaları:** alien invasions
- **doğal afet:** natural disaster
- **aklıma:** to my mind (dative)
- **etkileyen:** that effects (adjective)
- **tarihinizdeki:** in your history (plural/formal)
- **liderler:** leaders
- **yalnızca:** only
- **zaman:** then
- **büyük:** great
- **adam:** man
- **ulus:** nation
- **özgür:** free
- **borçluyuz:** we owe
- **her zaman:** always
- **hatırlıyoruz:** we remember
- **şanslı:** lucky
- **biziz:** we are
- **bir an önce:** right away, as soon as possible
- **bilgisayarını:** his computer (accusative)
- **olağanüstü:** amazing, fantastic
- **daha fazla bilgi:** more information
- **araştırma:** research

Questions about the story

1. Jack'in çalıştığı şirket, toplantı için onu İstanbul'a neden gönderdi?

   a) O, şirketin pazarlama müdürüdür.
   b) O, Türkçe konuşabiliyor.
   c) O, ayın elemanıdır.
   d) Jack'in anne ve babası Türk'tür.

2. Jack siren seslerini otele geri dönerken duydu. Doğru mu, yanlış mı?

   a) Doğru.
   b) Yanlış.

3. Siren seslerinin dışında Jack'i şaşırtan neydi?

   a) İnsanlar, arabalarını yolun sol tarafından sürüyorlardı.
   b) Dükkanlar kapalıydı.
   c) Trafik ışıkları çalışmıyordu.
   d) Sokaktaki herkes hareketsiz şekilde duruyordu.

4. Jack, Atatürk hakkında daha fazla şey öğrenmek ister. Doğru mu, yanlış mı?

   a) Doğru.
   b) Yanlış.

5. Türkler, Atatürk'ün vefatının yıl dönümünü ... tarihinde anarlar.

   a) 10 Temmuz.
   b) 10 Nisan.
   c) 10 Kasım.
   d) 10 Mart.

Answers

1) B – He can speak Turkish.
2) B – False.
3) D – Everyone on the street was standing still.
4) A – True.
5) C – November 10.

Chapter III

GİZEMLİ YAZAR — THE MYSTERIOUS WRİTER

Mehmet bir **bankada** çalışıyordu **fakat** çoğu **genç** adam gibi o da işini sevmezdi. Arkadaşlarına **sık sık** bu işin **ona göre** olmadığını söylerdi.

"**Yazar** olmak istiyorum. Bankadaki hayatla ilgili kitaplar yazamam, **hayatı** görmeliyim. **Başka** ülkelere gitmeli, oraların insanlarıyla **tanışmalıyım**," derdi.

Bankaya **yakın ufak** bir otelde kalıyordu. Otelde **bir sürü** insan vardı. **Akşam yemeği**ni yerken bu insanların çoğuyla tanışırdı. Kendisi pek **konuşkan** değildi ama **başkalarını dinlemeyi** çok severdi. **Bu şekilde** insanlar hakkında **birçok** şey öğrenirdi. Duyduklarını **odasında** sakladığı bir **deftere not ederdi**.

Bir gece, başına **ilginç** bir şey geldi. **Otelde** yemek yerken bir **adam** yanına **oturdu**. **Kocaman** mavi **gözleri** vardı. Mehmet adamın **yüzünü dikkatlice** inceledi, ona **sorular** sordu, kendisinden bahsetti:
— Bir bankada **çalışıyorum** ama orada **mutlu değilim**, dedi Mehmet.
— Bankada mı? **Güzel** bir iş, iyi **para** kazanıyorsunuzdur, değil mi? diye yanıtladı adam.
— **Evet, iyi kazanıyorum** ama **işimi** hiç sevmiyorum. Yazar olmak istiyorum.
— **Belki** size **yardım** edebilirim, ben yazarım.

Mehmet bunu duyunca çok **heyecanlandı**. Ona **mesleğiyle ilgili** sorular sormaya başladı:

— Kitap yazmaya **nasıl başlayabilirim**?

— İyi bildiğiniz **bir şey** hakkında **yazın**, dedi adam.

— Ama ben sadece **bankadaki hayatı** biliyorum. **Halk** bunu **okumak** istemez.

— **Her gün** bankanıza gelenleri **düşünün**! **Onlar** hakkında bir kitap yazabilirsiniz.

— **Nasıl** yapabilirim? Lütfen, bana söyleyin.

Adam **içki**sinden bir **yudum** aldı ve anlatmaya başladı:

— **İlk** hikayenizi yazmanız için size **yardım edeceğim**. **Çok sayıda** insan bankanıza geliyor. **Onlardan bazıları** çok zengin **müşteriler** olmalı. En zengini **kim**? diye sordu.

Mehmet biraz düşündükten sonra şöyle dedi:

— Öztürk Bey, **sanırım**. **En zengini** o; şehirde çok sayıda **dükkanı** var ve çok para kazanıyor.

— Bana onu **anlatın**. Öztürk Bey hakkındaki **her şeyi** anlatın, dedi adam.

— Öztürk Bey'in çok sayıda dükkanı ve **çalışanı** var. Ama zengin **görünmez**. Zengin insanlar **gibi** giyinmez, **elbiseleri** eskidir. **Her sabah** bankaya kendisi **gelir**. Dükkanlarından **parayı toplar** ve bankaya getirir. Parasını **daima** kirli, **eski** bir **çantanın içerisinde** taşır, diye anlattı Mehmet.

— **İşte** sizin hikayeniz. Onu **sizin için** yazamam ama **uğraşırsanız** Öztürk Bey hakkında **güzel** bir hikaye yazabilirsiniz, dedi adam.

— **Haklısınız. Yarın** Öztürk Bey hakkında bir hikaye yazmaya **başlayacağım**, dedi Mehmet.

Mehmet, yardımlarından dolayı adama **teşekkür etti** ve odasına gidip bazı **notlar aldı**.

Sabah uyandığında Mehmet, kendisini hiç **iyi hissetmiyordu**. Yatağından kalktı ve çalıştığı bankaya **telefon etti**:

— **Bugün** işe gelemeyeceğim. İyi değilim, dedi.

Öğleden sonra **iş arkadaşı** onu görmeye geldi.

— **Haberleri** duydun mu? diye sordu.

— Ne haberi? **Tüm gün** yataktaydım. **Hiçbir şey** duymadım.

— Öztürk Bey ile ilgili. **Bu sabah** bankaya gelirken bir adam ona saldırıp onun **tüm parasını çalmış.** Sonra da **koşarak** uzaklaşmış.

Mehmet bu habere çok **şaşırdı.**

— **Nasıl?** Kim? diye sordu.

— Öztürk Bey **dışında** kimse onu görmemiş. Adamın **yüzünde maske** varmış. Öztürk Bey'in tek hatırladığı, **hırsızın** mavi gözleri...

— **Mavi** gözler! dedi Mehmet. Yüzü bembeyaz oldu.

Birkaç gün **sonra,** Mehmet bankadaki **işinden ayrıldı.** Korktuğu için bu olaydan **kimseye** bahsedemedi. Hiç kimse bu "**gizemli** yazar"ın kim olduğunu **öğrenemedi.** Hırsız asla yakalanamadı. Fakat Mehmet'in **hayatı değişti.** Bir **hikaye kitabı** yazdı ve çok para kazandı. Hikayelerinden **en iyisi,** bankada çalışan genç bir adam hakkındaydı.

Hikayenin Özeti

Mehmet bir bankada çalışmaktadır fakat işini sevmez. Bir hayali vardır; yazar olmak. Bir gün otelde bir adamla tanışır. Adam, ona yazar olduğunu söyler. Mehmet bunun üzerine ondan tavsiye almak ister. Adam, Mehmet'ten bankasına gelen en zengin müşteriyi ona anlatmasını ister. Mehmet detaylarıyla anlatır ve adam ona bu müşteri hakkında hikaye yazabileceğini söyler.

Ertesi gün, Mehmet bankadaki o zengin müşterisine bir adamın saldırdığını, onun tüm parasını aldığını öğrenir. Bunu duyunca şok olur çünkü hırsız otelde tanıştığı o adamdır. Bu olaydan sonra Mehmet'in hayatı değişir.

Summary of the story

Mehmet works in a bank but he doesn't like his job. He has a dream: to be a writer. One day, he meets a man at the hotel. The man tells him that he is a writer. Then Mehmet wants to get advice from him. The man asks Mehmet to give him information about the richest customer in the bank. Mehmet describes in details and the man tells him that he can write a story about this customer.

The next day, Mehmet finds out that his rich customer has been attacked and all his money has been stolen. Mehmet get shocked to hear that because the thief is that man that he have met in the hotel last night. After this incident, Mehmet's life changes.

Vocabulary

- **bankada:** in bank (locative)
- **fakat:** but
- **genç:** young
- **sık sık:** often
- **ona göre:** for/according to him
- **yazar:** writer
- **hayatı:** the life (accusative)
- **başka:** other
- **tanışmalıyım:** I must meet
- **yakın:** close
- **ufak:** little
- **bir sürü:** many
- **akşam yemeği:** dinner
- **konuşkan:** talkative
- **başkalarını:** the others (accusative)
- **dinlemeyi:** listening (accusative)
- **bu şekilde:** thus, in this way
- **birçok:** many
- **odasında:** in his room (locative)
- **deftere:** notebook (dative)
- **not ederdi:** he was used to note down
- **bir gece:** one night
- **ilginç:** strange
- **otelde:** at the hotel (locative)
- **adam:** man
- **oturdu:** he sat
- **kocaman:** huge, big
- **gözleri:** his eyes
- **yüzünü:** his face (accusative)
- **dikkatlice:** carefully
- **sorular:** questions
- **çalışıyorum:** I am working
- **mutlu değilim:** I am not happy
- **güzel:** beautiful, good
- **para:** money
- **evet:** yes (interjection)
- **iyi kazanıyorum:** I am making good money
- **işimi:** my job (accusative)
- **belki:** maybe
- **yardım:** help
- **heyecanlandı:** he got excited
- **mesleğiyle ilgili:** about his job
- **kitap:** book

- **nasıl başlayabilirim:** how can I start
- **bir şey:** something
- **yazın:** write (imperative, plural/formal)
- **bankadaki hayatı:** the life at the bank (accusative)
- **halk:** the people
- **okumak:** to read (infinitive)
- **her gün:** every day
- **düşünün:** think about (imperative)
- **onlar:** they/them
- **nasıl:** how
- **içki:** drink
- **yudum:** sip
- **ilk:** the first
- **yardım edeceğim:** I will help
- **çok sayıda:** many
- **onlardan bazıları:** some of them (possessive)
- **müşteriler:** customers
- **kim:** who
- **sanırım:** I suppose
- **en zengini:** the richest of (possessive)
- **dükkan:** store
- **anlatın:** you tell (imperative, plural/formal)
- **her şeyi:** everything
- **çalışanı:** his employee (possessive)
- **görünmez:** he doesn't look
- **gibi:** like
- **elbiseleri:** his clothes (possessive)
- **her sabah:** every morning
- **gelir:** he comes
- **parayı toplar:** he collects the money
- **daima:** always
- **eski:** old
- **çantanın içerisinde:** in the bag (locative)
- **işte:** here
- **sizin için:** for you (plural/formal)
- **uğraşırsanız:** if you work hard (plural/formal)
- **güzel:** good, beautiful
- **haklısınız:** you are right (plural/formal)
- **yarın:** tomorrow
- **başlayacağım:** I am going to start
- **teşekkür etti:** he thanked
- **notlar aldı:** he took notes
- **sabah:** morning
- **iyi hissetmiyordu:** he wasn't feeling well
- **telefon etti:** he called

- **bugün:** today
- **iş arkadaşı:** his colleague
- **haberleri:** the news (accusative)
- **tüm gün:** all day
- **hiçbir şey:** nothing
- **bu sabah:** this morning
- **tüm parasını:** all his money (accusative)
- **çalmış:** he had stolen
- **koşarak:** running (adverb)
- **şaşırdı:** he was surprised
- **nasıl:** how
- **dışında:** except, but
- **yüzünde:** on his face (locative)

- **maske:** mask
- **hırsızın:** thief's (possessive)
- **mavi:** blue
- **sonra:** then
- **işinden ayrıldı:** he quit his job
- **kimseye:** to no one (dative)
- **gizemli:** mysterious
- **öğrenemedi:** he couldn't find out
- **hayatı değişti:** his life changed
- **hikaye kitabı:** story book
- **en iyisi:** the best of (possessive)

Questions about the story

1. **Hikayeye göre Mehmet'in en büyük hayali...**

   a) Fakirlere yardım etmek.

   b) Yazar olmak.

   c) Büyük bir ev almak.

   d) Bankacı olmak.

2. **Oteldeki adam ona ... ile ilgili hikaye yazmasını tavsiye ediyor.**

   a) Bankacılığın zorlukları.

   b) Çocukluk anıları.

   c) Bankadaki en zengin müşteri.

   d) Patronu.

3. **Mehmet hırsızı nasıl tanıyor?**

   a) Konuşmasından.

   b) Yüzündeki yara izinden.

   c) Gözlerinden.

   d) Sakalından.

4. **Mehmet tüm bu olaylardan sonra işten ayrılıyor. Doğru mu, yanlış mı?**

   a) Doğru.

   b) Yanlış.

5. **Mehmet'in en iyi hikayesi neyi konu alıyor?**

   a) Küresel ekonomik sorunları.

   b) Dünyanın en zengin insanlarını.

   c) Bankada çalışan genç bir adamı.

   d) Müşterilerle ilişkilerini.

Answers

1) B – To be a writer
2) C – The richest customer in the bank.
3) C – By his eyes.
4) A – True.
5) C – A young man working in a bank.

Chapter IV

BU KİMİN KÖPEĞİ? —
WHOSE DOG IS THİS?

Yalçın **Bey**, **şehir dışında** büyük bir evde yaşıyordu. **Oldukça** zengin bir adamdı ve çalışmaya ihtiyacı yoktu. Avlanmak, **balık tutmak** onun en büyük hobilerinden biriydi. Evinin bulunduğu **araziden** bir **nehir** geçiyordu ve **genellikle** burada balık tutuyordu.

Bir gün arazide **yürürken** nehrin **kıyısında** bir adam gördü. Adam balık tutuyordu. Yalçın Bey, adamı görünce çok **sinirlendi**. "Balıklarımı **çalıyor**!" diye düşündü.

Adama **doğru koştu**.
— **Bırak**! Burada **ne yapıyorsun**? diye bağırdı.
— Balık tutuyorum **efendim**, dedi adam.
— Burası benim arazim. **Dolayısıyla** nehrin **bu bölümü** bana **ait**. Buradaki **balıklar** da…
— Ama nehirde **bir sürü** balık var, **hepsini** tutmadım, dedi adam şaşkınlıkla.
— **Fark etmez**! Nehrin bana ait olan bölümünde balık tutuyorsun. Sen bir **hırsızsın**! dedi Yalçın Bey.
— **Hayır** efendim. Ben hırsız **değilim**. Bu balıklar nehrin **diğer tarafına** gidiyorlar. **Burada** yaşamıyorlar. **O yüzden** size ait olamazlar, dedi adam.
— Nehrin **bu bölümünde** oldukları **sürece** onlar **benim** balıklarım, diye **cevap verdi** Yalçın Bey.
— **Peki** efendim. Balıkları **tekrar** nehre **atacağım**.

— Hayır. Onları **bana ver**, eve götüreceğim.

Adam **tuttuğu balıkları** Yalçın Bey'e verdi.

— Senin **adın** ne? diye sordu Yalçın Bey.

— İsmim Hasan, diye cevap verdi adam.

— Hasan, **bir daha** buraya gelme. Seni tekrar burada görürsem **polis çağıracağım**. Nehrin bu bölümü bana ait. Benim balıklarımı **tutamazsın**.

Hasan **üzgün** bir şekilde evin yolunu tuttu.

Birkaç ay sonra Yalçın Bey, **arazisinde köpeğini** gezdirmeye çıktı. Ama köpek **kaçtı** ve geri **dönmedi. Her tarafta** aramasına **rağmen** köpeği **bulamadı**. Bunun üzerine polise **haber verdi** ve köpeğinin bulunmasını **istedi**.

— Köpeğimizi **kaybettik**. Bize **yardımcı olur musunuz?** Büyük, **beyaz** bir köpekti.

— Yalçın Bey, köpeğinizin **daha hızlı** bulunması için bulan **kişiye para** vermek **istiyor musunuz?** diye sordu polis memuru.

Yalçın Bey **biraz** düşündü. Zengin bir adamdı ama **para harcamak**tan hoşlanmazdı.

— Evet, 50 lira **vereceğim**, dedi.

— 50 lira **verirsen** onu **asla** bulamayız, dedi eşi.

Eşi çok üzgün görünüyordu. **Köpeği** çok seviyordu.

— **Tamam**, 500 lira vereceğim **o halde**. Ama **lütfen** köpeğimi bulun, dedi Yalçın Bey.

— **Elimizden geleni yapacağız**, diye yanıtladı polis memuru.

Aradan günler **geçti**. Yalçın Bey, her gün **polis karakolu**nu arayıp köpeğini **bulup bulamadıklarını** soruyordu. Ama **her defasında** aynı yanıtı alıyordu. Bir **sabah**, polis memurlarından **biri** onu aradı ve köpeğinin **bulunduğunu** söyledi.

— **Harika**! Benim **hanım** çok sevinecek. Onu **ne zaman** getireceksiniz? diye sordu Yalçın Bey.

— **Üzgünüm.** Köpeğinizi getiremeyiz.

— Anlamadım. **Neden**?

— Yalçın Bey, bu sabah bir **köylü**nün yanında sizin köpeğinize **benzer** bir köpek gördük. Sizin köpeğiniz olduğunu **düşündük** ve adama sorduk. Adam "**Hayır**, bu benim köpeğim." dedi. **İsterseniz** sizi bu adamla görüştürebiliriz.

Yalçın Bey, adamla **görüşmek** istediğini söyledi. Polislerden adamın **nerede oturduğunu** öğrendi. **Heyecan** içindeydi çünkü köpeğini çok **özlemişti**. Kendisine verilen **adres**e gitti. Burası bahçesi **küçük olan** bir **ev**di ve içeriden bir köpeğin **havlama sesi** geliyordu. Sesi **hemen** tanıdı, **kapıyı çaldı**.

Kapıyı açan adam **bahçeye** çıktı. Hasan'dı bu.

— **Tahmin** etmeliydim, köpeğimi sen çaldın **demek ki**, dedi Yalçın Bey.

Hasan **gülümsedi**.

— Köpek senin evinde **kalırken sana aitti**. Ama **artık değil** çünkü benim evimde yaşamaya **geldi**. Bir akşam, baktım ki bahçemde **oturuyor**. Bu yüzden o **artık** benim köpeğim.

Yalçın bey **öfkeyle** Hasan'a baktı. Bir şey söylemek için **ağzını açtı**. Sonra **durdu**, biraz düşündü ve **sessizce** oradan **uzaklaştı**.

Hikayenin Özeti

Yalçın Bey, balık tutmayı çok seven zengin bir adamdır. Bir gün, evinin yakınlarında balık tutan bir adam görür. İsmi Hasan'dır. Hasan'ı balıklarını çalmakla suçlar çünkü nehrin o bölümü ve balıklar kendisine aittir. Ona bir daha oraya gelmemesini söyler.

Birkaç ay sonra, Yalçın Bey'in köpeği kaybolur. Her yerde köpeğini arar ama bulamaz. Polislerden köpeğini bulmasını ister. Bir gün, polisler Yalçın Bey'i ararlar ve ona köpeğinin bulunduğunu söylerler. Köpeği bir adam bulmuştur fakat köpeğin kendisine ait olduğunu iddia ediyordu. Bunun üzerine Yalçın Bey, köpeğini almak için adamın evine gider. Bu adam, birkaç ay önce evinin yakınında balık tutan Hasan'dır. Yalçın Bey, köpeğini geri ister fakat Hasan, ona köpeğin artık onun evinde yaşadığını, dolayısıyla kendisine ait olduğunu söyler.

Summary of the story

Mr. Yalçın is a rich man who enjoys fishing. One day, he sees a man fishing near his house. His name is Hasan. He accuses Hasan of stealing his fishes because that part of the river belongs to him, so do the fishes. He tells the man not to come there again.

A few months later, Mr. Yalçın's dog goes missing. He looks for his dog everywhere but he can't find. He asks the police to find his dog. One day, the police gives him a call and tells that his dog has been found. A man has found it but he claims that it's his dog. Then, Mr. Yalçın goes to his house to get his dog back. This man is Hasan, the man who has been fishing near his home a few months ago. Mr. Yalçın wants his dog back, but Hasan tells him that the dog now lives in his house and therefore belongs to him.

Vocabulary

- **bey:** Mr.
- **şehir:** town
- **dışında:** out, outside (locative)
- **oldukça:** quite, very
- **balık tutmak:** to angle, to fish (infinitive)
- **araziden:** land (ablative)
- **nehir:** river
- **genellikle:** usually
- **bir gün:** on day
- **yürürken:** when he was walking
- **kıyısında:** on bank (locative) [on the river bank]
- **sinirlendi:** he got mad
- **çalıyor:** he is stealing
- **doğru:** towards
- **koştu:** he ran
- **bırak:** stop (imperative)
- **ne yapıyorsun:** what are you doing
- **efendim:** sir
- **dolayısıyla:** so, therefore
- **bu bölümü:** that part (accusative)
- **ait:** belong
- **balıklar:** fish (plural)
- **bir sürü:** plenty
- **hepsini:** all of them (accusative)
- **fark etmez:** it doesn't matter
- **hırsızsın:** you are thief
- **hayır:** no (interjection)
- **değilim:** I am not
- **diğer tarafına:** to other side (dative)
- **burada:** here (locative)
- **yüzden:** thus
- **bu bölümünde:** in this part (locative)
- **sürece:** as long as
- **benim:** my, mine
- **cevap verdi:** he replied
- **peki:** alright
- **tekrar:** again
- **atacağım:** I'll throw
- **bana ver:** give me (imperative)
- **tuttuğu balıkları:** the fish that he caught (accusative)
- **adın:** your name
- **bir daha:** again, once more
- **polis:** police

- **çağıracağım:** I'll call
- **tutamazsın:** you can't catch
- **üzgün:** sad
- **birkaç ay:** couple months
- **arazisinde:** in his land (locative)
- **köpeğini:** his dog (accusative)
- **kaçtı:** it ran away
- **dönmedi:** it didn't come back
- **her tarafta:** all over, everywhere (locative)
- **rağmen:** despite, although
- **bulamadı:** he couldn't find
- **haber verdi:** he informed
- **istedi:** he asked
- **kaybettik:** we lost
- **yardımcı olur musunuz:** can you help (plural/formal)
- **beyaz:** white
- **daha hızlı:** faster
- **kişiye:** to the person (dative)
- **para:** money
- **istiyor musunuz:** do you want (plural/formal)
- **polis memuru:** police officer
- **biraz:** for a while
- **para harcamak:** spending money (infinitive)
- **vereceğim:** I will give
- **verirsen:** if you give
- **asla:** never
- **eşi:** his wife (possessive)
- **köpeği:** the dog (accusative)
- **tamam:** OK (interjection)
- **halde:** then
- **lütfen:** please (interjection)
- **elimizden geleni yapacağız:** we will do our best
- **geçti:** it passed
- **polis karakolu:** police station
- **bulup bulamadıklarını:** whether they could find or not (accusative)
- **her defasında:** every time
- **sabah:** morning
- **biri:** one of/somebody
- **bulunduğunu:** that it has been found (accusative)
- **harika:** great
- **benim hanım:** my wife
- **ne zaman:** when
- **üzgünüm:** I'm sorry
- **neden:** why
- **köylü:** villager

- **benzer:** similar
- **düşündük:** we thought
- **hayır:** no (interjection)
- **isterseniz:** if you want (plural/formal)
- **görüşmek:** to meet (infinitive)
- **nerede oturduğunu:** where he lives (accusative)
- **heyecan:** excitement
- **özlemişti:** he missed
- **adres:** adress
- **küçük:** little
- **olan:** with/that has (adjective)
- **ev:** house
- **havlama sesi:** bark
- **hemen:** immediately
- **kapıyı çaldı:** he knocked the door

- **bahçeye:** garden (dative)
- **tahmin:** guess
- **demek ki:** so, it means
- **gülümsedi:** he smiled
- **kalırken:** when it was staying
- **sana aitti:** it belonged to you
- **artık değil:** no longer
- **geldi:** it came
- **oturuyor:** it is sitting
- **artık:** now
- **öfkeyle:** with anger
- **ağzını açtı:** he opened his mouth
- **durdu:** he stopped
- **sessizce:** quietly
- **uzaklaştı:** he walked away

Questions about the story

1. **Yalçın Bey, balıkların ona ait olduğunu iddia eder çünkü...**

   a) Kendisi balıkçıdır.
   b) Nehrin bu bölümündeki balıkları o besler.
   c) Arazisinde yabancıları istemez.
   d) Nehrin bu bölümü onun arazisinden geçer.

2. **Yalçın Bey parasını başkalarıyla paylaşmayı sever. Doğru mu, yanlış mı?**

   a) Doğru.
   b) Yanlış.

3. **Yalçın Bey, köpeğini kaybettikten sonra ne yaptı?**

   a) Arazisine Hasan'ın girmesine izin verdi.
   b) Yeni bir köpek aldı.
   c) Polislerden yardım istedi.
   d) Hasan'dan intikam almak istedi.

4. **Hasan tuttuğu balıkları nehre geri attı. Doğru mu, yanlış mı?**

   a) Doğru.
   b) Yanlış.

5. **Hasan köpeği geri vermez çünkü ...**

   a) Köpek onun evinde kalmayı seçmiştir.
   b) Köpek yaralıdır.
   c) Onun çocukları köpeği çok sever.
   d) Yalçın Bey'den nefret eder.

Answers

1) D – That part of the river goes through his land.
2) B – False.
3) C – He asked the cops for help.
4) B – False.
5) A – The dog has chosen his house to stay.

Chapter V

AV — HUNTİNG

Akşam yemeği sırasında Hakan hiç **konuşmuyordu. Annesinin** koyduğu yemeği **bile** yiyemiyordu. İçinde bir **sıkıntı** vardı. O akşam, **amcası elinde av tüfeğiyle** eve gelmişti. **Ertesi sabah** ava gideceklerdi.

Dışarı çıkacaklar ve **gördükleri** herhangi bir hayvanı **öldüreceklerdi.** Birçok kez **yalvarmıştı** amcasına:

— **Lütfen,** gitmeyelim. **Hayvanları** öldürmeyelim!

Amcası bu sözlere **gülmüştü.**

— **Av** bir **spor**dur. **Amaç,** zevk almaktır. **Ayrıca, doğada** av olanlar da vardır, **avcılar** da... **Hayatın düzeni** budur, demişti.

Hakan, amcasının bu **sözlerini** ve öldürecekleri **masum** hayvanları düşünüyordu. **Birden** kalktı, odasına **koştu. Yatağına** uzandı ve **ağlamaya** başladı.

Gece yarısı ailesi uyuduktan **sonra** yataktan kalktı. **Onun dışında** herkes uykudaydı. **Sessizce** salona **girdi. Kimse**nin uyanmasını istemediği için **ışıkları** açmadı. Salonda **içerisinde** iki **muhabbet kuşu** bulunan bir **kafes** duruyordu. Kafesi **dikkatli bir şekilde** aldı ve **balkon zeminine** bıraktı.

— **Lütfen** beni **affedin!** Sizi **çok** seviyorum ama beni bunu **yapmaya zorladılar,** diyerek konuştu **kuşlarla.**

Kafesi **orada bıraktı** ve sessizce odasına **geri döndü.**

Sabaha karşı evde çok **gürültülü** bir ses **duyuldu.** Düşen, **parçalanan** bir şeyin **sesi** ve **tiz** çığlıklar... Minik kuşların **son çığlıklarıydı** bu sesler. Hakan, hemen **salona** koştu. Ailesi salonda **toplanmıştı**, ne olduğunu **anlamaya çalışıyordu.**

— **Kim** açık bıraktı **bu kapıyı**? diye **bağırdı** babası.

— Kuşlar! **Kuşlarım!** dedi annesi.

Hasan'ın amcası **elinde tüfeğiyle** salona koşmuştu.

— Nerede o **hırsız**? **Kaçtı** mı? diye sordu.

Annesi **yanındaki** koltuğa **oturdu** ve ağlamaya başladı.

— Hırsız değil, **kediler!** Kafesi **parçalamışlar. Zavallı** minik kuşlarım...

Amcasının **yüzü** öfkeden **kıpkırmızı olmuştu.**

— **Nerede** onlar! diyerek kapıya yöneldi.

Hakan, bunu **duyar duymaz** amcasının yanına koştu.

— **Ne oldu** amca? Nereye? diye sordu.

— O kedileri **geberteceğim**, diye yanıtladı amcası.

— Neden?

— Sen benimle **dalga mı geçiyorsun**? Kedilerin yaptığına **bak!** Kuşlarımızı **öldürdüler** ve kalkmış neden diye **soruyorsun!** dedi amcası öfkeyle.

— Kediler **suçlu** mu? **Neden** onlara kızıyorsun? Kediler **karınlarını doyurmak** için **avlanmak zorunda.** Biz avlanmak zorunda olmadığımız **halde** masum hayvanları öldürmek için ava gitmeyi **planlıyoruz. Doğası gereği** kuşa saldıran bir kediyi **nasıl suçlarım?**

Hakan **bir süre** sustu, amcasının o akşam söylediklerini **hatırlamaya** çalıştı.

— Hem senin de **dediğin gibi**, hayatın düzeni bu, değil mi? diye sordu.

Amcası **bir anda** şaşkınlığa uğradı. **Dudaklarını kıpırdattı** fakat konuşamadı.

— Ben... diyebildi **sadece.**

Çocuk **haklıydı.** Söylenecek bir şey yoktu. Sabahki av planını **iptal etmeye karar verdi.**

Hikayenin Özeti

Hakan, hayvanları seven bir çocuktur. Bir akşam, amcası eve gelir ve ertesi gün ava çıkacaklarını söyler. Hakan buna çok üzülür çünkü masum hayvanları öldüreceklerdir. Aklına bir plan gelir. Herkes uyuduktan sonra evlerinde besledikleri kuşların kafesini balkona çıkarır. Sabaha karşı, evdekiler büyük bir gürültüyle uyanır ve kedilerin kuşlara saldırdığını fark ederler. Hakan'ın amcası çok öfkelenir, tüfeğini kapıp o kedileri öldürmek ister. Fakat Hakan, amcasını durdurur ve ona akşam yemekte söylediği sözleri hatırlatır.

Summary of the story

Hakan is a kid who loves animals. One evening, her uncle comes home and tells that they will go hunting on the following day. Hakan gets very upset because they will kill innocent animals. He comes up with a plan. After everyone falls asleep, he takes the cage of the birds that they feed at home into the balcony. In the morning, the people at home are woken by a loud noise and realize that cats have attacked the birds. Hakan's uncle gets mad, takes his rifle and wants to kill the cats. However, Hakan stops him and reminds him his words that he said at the dinner.

Vocabulary

- **akşam yemeği:** dinner
- **konuşmuyordu:** he was not talking
- **annesinin:** his mom's (possessive)
- **bile:** even
- **sıkıntı:** distress, unease
- **amcası:** his uncle
- **elinde:** in his hand (locative)
- **av tüfeğiyle:** with shotgun
- **ertesi sabah:** next morning
- **dışarı:** out, outside
- **gördükleri:** that they see
- **öldüreceklerdi:** they would kill
- **yalvarmıştı:** he had begged
- **lütfen:** please (interjection)
- **hayvanları:** animals (accusative)
- **gülmüştü:** he had laughed
- **av:** hunting
- **spor:** sport
- **amaç:** goal, purpose
- **ayrıca:** besides, additionally
- **doğada:** in nature (locative)
- **avcılar:** hunters
- **hayatın düzeni:** life's order
- **sözlerini:** his words (accusative)
- **masum:** innocent
- **birden:** suddenly
- **koştu:** he ran
- **yatağına:** to his bed (dative)
- **ağlamaya:** crying (dative)
- **gece yarısı:** midnight
- **sonra:** after
- **onun dışında:** except him
- **sessizce:** silently
- **girdi:** he entered
- **kimse:** no one
- **ışıkları:** lights (accusative)
- **içerisinde:** inside (locative)
- **muhabbet kuşu:** lovebird
- **kafes:** cage
- **dikkatli bir şekilde:** carefully
- **balkon:** balcony
- **zeminine:** on/to the floor (dative)
- **lütfen:** please (interjection)
- **affedin:** you forgive (plural/formal)

- **çok:** so much
- **yapmaya zorladılar:** they forced to do
- **kuşlarla:** with birds
- **orada:** there (locative)
- **bıraktı:** he left
- **geri döndü:** he turned back
- **sabaha karşı:** at dawn, towards morning
- **gürültülü:** loud
- **duyuldu:** it was heard
- **parçalanan:** broken (adjective)
- **sesi:** voice of (possessive)
- **tiz:** shrill
- **son:** the last
- **çığlıklar:** screams
- **salona:** to living room (dative)
- **toplanmıştı:** he/she gathered
- **anlamaya çalışıyordu:** he/she was trying to figure out
- **kim:** who
- **bu kapıyı:** that door (accusative)
- **bağırdı:** he yelled
- **kuşlarım:** my birds
- **elinde tüfeğiyle:** with his shotgun in his hand
- **hırsız:** thief
- **kaçtı:** he ran away
- **yanındaki:** next to her
- **koltuğa:** on couch (dative)
- **oturdu:** she sat
- **kediler:** cats
- **parçalamışlar:** they smashed
- **zavallı:** poor
- **yüzü:** his face
- **kıpkırmızı:** red
- **olmuştu:** it has turned
- **nerede:** where (locative)
- **duyar duymaz:** as soon as he heard
- **ne oldu:** what happened
- **gebereceğim:** I will kill
- **dalga mı geçiyorsun:** are you kidding
- **bak:** look (imperative)
- **öldürdüler:** they killed
- **soruyorsun:** you are asking
- **suçlu:** guilty
- **neden:** why
- **karınlarını doyurmak:** to eat their fill (infinitive)
- **avlanmak zorunda:** it has to hunt
- **halde:** even though
- **planlıyoruz:** we are planning

- **doğası gereği:** by its nature
- **nasıl suçlarım:** how can I blame
- **bir süre:** for a while
- **hatırlamaya:** to remember (dative)
- **dediğin gibi:** as you said
- **bir anda:** at once
- **dudaklarını:** his lips (accusative)
- **kıpırdattı:** he moved
- **sadece:** just
- **haklıydı:** he was right
- **iptal etmeye:** to cancel (dative)
- **karar verdi:** he decided

Questions about the story

1. **Hakan, akşam yemeğinde çok mutsuzdur çünkü ...**

    a) Amcasıyla kavga etmiştir.

    b) Ertesi gün ava gideceklerdir.

    c) Ailesi çok fakirdir ve babası işten çıkmıştır.

    d) Kafeste besledikleri kuşlardan biri ölmüştür.

2. **Hakan'ın amcası av ile ilgili ne düşünür?**

    a) Av bir spordur.

    b) Hayatta kalmaları için avlanmaları gerekmektedir.

    c) Masum hayvanları öldürmeye gerek yoktur.

    d) Yeni aldığı tüfeği, bir hayvan üzerinde denemek ister.

3. **Hakan, amcasını ikna etmek için ne yapar?**

    a) Amcasının tüfeğini saklar.

    b) Evi terk eder.

    c) Kafesteki kuşları kurban eder.

    d) Babasından yardım ister.

4. **Hakan, kuşların kafesini balkona çıkarır. Doğru mu, yanlış mı?**

    a) Doğru.

    b) Yanlış.

5. **Kuşların ölümünün üzerine amcası ...**

    a) Kedileri vurur.

    b) Av planını iptal eder.

    c) Kuşlarından ölümünden Hakan'ı sorumlu tutar.

    d) Tüfeğini satar.

Answers

1) B – They will go hunting the next day.
2) A – Hunting is a sport.
3) C – He sacrifices the birds in the cage.
4) A – True.
5) B – He cancels the hunting plan.

Chapter VI

AŞK MI PARA MI? — LOVE OR MONEY?

Oktay, **deniz kıyısında** oturmuş uzaklardaki **dalgaları** seyrediyordu. **Güzel** bir gündü, deniz **masmaviydi**; ama Oktay hiç **mutlu** değildi. **Hayatını** düşünüyordu. "**Yaşlanıyorum.**" diye düşündü. "Çok çalışmam **gerekiyor** ama ben yaşlanıyorum. Çok param olmalı **yoksa** hanım beni **terk edecek.** Beni **artık** sevmiyor." dedi.

Eşine baktı. **Hâlâ** güzel bir **kadındı** ve onu çok seviyordu. Evliliklerinin **ilk yıllarını**, çocuklarının **küçük** olduğu ve fazla paraları olmadığı **zamanları** düşündü. **Ne kadar** mutluydular!

İlk evlerini **satın almak için** çok çalışmıştı. **Yıllar boyunca** işinde ilerledi, **kendisi için** çalışan **bir sürü** insana sahip oldu; **fakat** bu, onun için daha fazla iş **yarattı.** Her şeyle ilgilenmek ve **diğer adamlara** da işi **öğretmek** zorunda kaldı. Zamanla **daha büyük** bir ev ve daha büyük bir **araba** satın aldılar. Eşi sürekli **yeni kıyafetler** istemeye başladı. Oktay bunu hiç anlamıyordu çünkü **eskiden** eşi **kendi elbiselerini** kendisi **dikerdi.**

Eşi, okuduğu **kitaptan** başını kaldırdı.

— Bu ay **biraz daha fazla** para kazanman gerek, dedi.

— Neden? diye sordu Oktay.

— Birkaç elbise **gördüm**, onları **alacağım.**

— Ama bir sürü elbisen var **zaten.** Neden daha **fazlasını** istiyorsun?

— Diğerleri **eski.** Artık bana **yakışmıyorlar.**

— **Bence** çok yakışıyorlar, eski de değiller, diye yanıtladı Oktay.

Eşi sinirlenmeye başlamıştı.

— **Erkekler,** kadın giysilerinden anlamazlar, bunu sana **hep söylüyorum.**

— Onların parasını **ödemek zorunda olan** benim, **sen değilsin.**

— Paran var, **zenginsin. Elbette** eşine **yeni** giysiler alabilirsin.

— O parayı **elde etmek** için çok çalışmak zorundayım. Bunu **biliyorsun.**

Eşi **hiçbir şey** söylemedi. Kitabını okumaya **devam etti.** Oktay, masmavi **denize** ve **kıyıya vuran dalgalara** baktı.

"**Artık** benim **ne hissettiğimin** hiç **önemi yok. Onun için** önemli olan **tek şey** yeni giysilere, eşyalara **sahip olmak.** Hayatında ben olmasam **bile fark etmez.** Belki de **daha iyi** olur. **Böylece** bütün **paramız** ona kalmış olur ve kendine **istediği her şeyi** alabilir. Beni **zaten** umursamayacaktır. **Kısa süre sonra** da **tamamen** unutacaktır." diye düşündü. Ayağa kalktı.

— **Denize gireceğim,** dedi.

— Su çok **soğuk.** Girmesen iyi olur, diye yanıtladı eşi.

— **Sorun değil.** Soğuk suyu seviyorum.

— **Yaşlanıyorsun.** Bu kadar soğuk suya girersen **hasta** olursun. Elbiselerini **giy,** otele **geri dönmek** istiyorum.

— Sen **dönebilirsin,** ben gireceğim, dedi Oktay.

— **Nasıl istersen.** Fakat çok kalma, **dükkanları** dolaşmak istiyorum.

Oktay suya girdi. **Sinirlenmişti** ve çok üzgündü. Eşi neden böyle **davranıyordu? Hiçbir zaman** mutlu olmuyor ve **her zaman** bir şeyler istiyordu. Hızla **yüzmeye** devam etti. Dünyadan **yok olsa** eşinin neler **hissedeceğini** düşünüyordu. Biraz üzülürdü **belki de.** Şaşırırdı. Onu böyle **panik** içinde **hayal etmek** hoşuna gitti birden. Daha da **uzaklaştı kıyıdan.** Ama sonra **birden** korkmaya başladı. **Durdu,** kıyıya baktı. Her şey ne kadar **uzaktaydı.**

51

— **İmdat!** diye bağırdı. Çok korkmuştu.

— İmdat! Lütfen **biri beni kurtarsın!**

Yakınlarda iki adam, bir **balıkçı kayığında** balık tutuyordu. Oktay'ın **bağırışlarını** duyduktan sonra hemen **oraya** gittiler. Onu kayığa **çektiler**, ona yiyecek bir şeyler **verdiler**. Oktay çok **üşümüş** ve **yorulmuştu**. Fakat sudan çıkmayı **başarmıştı**, başka hiçbir şey umurunda değildi. Bunları düşünürken bir anda **gözleri** kapandı. Oracıkta **bayıldı**.

Gözlerini **açtığında** otel odasındaki yatağındaydı. Eşi, yatağın **kenarında** oturuyordu, ağlıyordu.

— Neden ağlıyorsun? diye sordu Oktay.

— **Ölebilirdin!** Çok korktum! dedi eşi.

— Ölmek **istedim**, diye yanıtladı.

— Neden? Her şeye **sahipsin**. Neden ölmek istedin?

— Artık değilim. Sen beni artık **sevmiyorsun**.

— **Neden** böyle söylüyorsun? Seni **tabii ki** seviyorum, bunu **biliyorsun**, dedi eşi.

— Eskiden severdin. Şimdi **yalnızca paramı** seviyorsun. Ben, senin için elbiselerinin **parasını veren** adamım sadece.

— **Hayır!** Seni seviyorum! Güzel giysiler almak istiyorum **çünkü** senin **eşinim**. Sana **güzel görünmek** istiyorum. Artık **eskisi gibi** genç ve güzel değilim. Yeni elbiseleri **bu yüzden** istiyorum.

— Sen **bütün** elbiselerin **içinde** çok güzelsin, dedi Oktay.

Eşi ona baktı ve **genç** bir kız gibi heyecanla gülümsedi.

— **Bunu** neden bana daha önce **söylemedin**?

— **Bilmiyorum**, dedi Oktay.

Hikayenin Özeti

Oktay çok mutsuzdur çünkü eşinin artık onu sevmediğini düşünür. Yaşlanıyordur ve eskisi kadar para kazanması için çok çalışması gerekmektedir. Eşi ondan sürekli yeni kıyafetler almasını istediği için Oktay'ın paraya ihtiyacı vardır. Oktay'a göre eşi, onunla parası için birliktedir artık. Denize girmek ve orada ölmek ister. Fakat birden büyük bir korkuya kapılır. İki balıkçı onu kurtarır fakat Oktay bayılır.

Oktay gözünü otel odasında açar. Eşi bunu neden yaptığını sorduğunda Oktay eşinin artık onu sevmediğini, bu yüzden ölmek istediğini söyler. Eşi onu çok sevdiğini, yeni giysileri ona güzel görünmek için istediğini söyler.

Summary of the story

Oktay is very unhappy because he thinks that his wife doesn't like him anymore. He is getting old and he needs to work hard to earn much more money than before. He needs money because his wife always wants him to buy new clothes for her. To Oktay, his wife is with him for his money. He wants to get into the sea and die there. However, he is seized with a great fear suddenly. Two fishermen save him but Oktay faints.

He opens his eyes in the hotel room. When his wife asks him why he has done this, Oktay says that his wife no longer loves him, so he wanted to die. His wife says that she loves him very much and she wants new clothes to look beautiful for her husband.

Vocabulary

- **deniz kıyısında:** by the sea (locative)
- **dalgaları:** waves (accusative)
- **güzel:** beautiful
- **masmaviydi:** it was deep blue
- **mutlu:** happy
- **hayatını:** his life (accusative)
- **yaşlanıyorum:** I am getting old
- **gerekiyor:** I need
- **yoksa:** or, otherwise
- **terk edecek:** she will leave me
- **artık:** anymore
- **eşine:** his wife (dative)
- **hâlâ:** still
- **kadın:** woman
- **ilk yıllarını:** first years (accusative)
- **küçük:** little
- **zamanları:** the times (accusative)
- **ne kadar:** how
- **satın almak için:** in order to buy
- **yıllar:** years
- **boyunca:** throughout
- **kendisi için:** for him
- **bir sürü:** plenty
- **fakat:** but
- **yarattı:** it created
- **diğer adamlara:** to other men (dative)
- **öğretmek:** to teach (infinitive)
- **daha büyük:** bigger
- **araba:** car
- **yeni kıyafetler:** new clothes
- **eskiden:** before
- **kendi elbiselerini:** her own clothes (accusative)
- **dikerdi:** she used to sew
- **kitaptan:** the book (ablative)
- **biraz daha:** some more
- **gördüm:** I saw
- **alacağım:** I'll buy
- **zaten:** already
- **fazlasını:** more (accusative)
- **eski:** old

- **yakışmıyorlar:** they don't fit
- **bence:** I think, in my opinion
- **erkekler:** men
- **hep:** always
- **söylüyorum:** I am saying
- **ödemek zorunda olan:** the one who has to pay
- **sen değilsin:** you are not
- **zenginsin:** you are rich
- **elbette:** of course
- **yeni:** new
- **elde etmek:** to get/to obtain (infinitive)
- **biliyorsun:** you know
- **hiçbir şey:** nothing
- **devam etti:** she continued
- **denize:** sea (dative)
- **kıyıya vuran:** washing up on the shore
- **dalgalara:** waves (dative)
- **artık:** anymore
- **ne hissettiğimin:** of how I feel (possessive)
- **önemi yok:** it doesn't matter
- **onun için:** to her, for her
- **tek şey:** only thing
- **sahip olmak:** to have (infinitive)
- **bile:** even if
- **fark etmez:** it doesn't matter
- **daha iyi:** better
- **böylece:** so
- **paramız:** our money
- **istediği:** that she wants
- **her şeyi:** everything (accusative)
- **zaten:** anyway
- **kısa süre sonra:** soon, after a short while
- **tamamen:** completely
- **denize gireceğim:** I'll go into the sea
- **soğuk:** cold
- **sorun değil:** no problem
- **yaşlanıyorsun:** you are getting old
- **hasta:** sick
- **giy:** put on (imperative)
- **geri dönmek:** to go back (infinitive)
- **dönebilirsin:** you can go back
- **nasıl istersen:** as you wish
- **dükkanları:** the stores (accusative)
- **sinirlenmişti:** he got mad

- **davranıyordu:** she was acting
- **hiçbir zaman:** never
- **her zaman:** always
- **yüzmeye:** to swim (dative)
- **yok olsa:** if he disappears
- **hissedeceğini:** that she will feel (accusative)
- **belki de:** maybe
- **panik:** panic
- **hayal etmek:** to imagine (infinitive)
- **uzaklaştı:** he strayed far/moved away
- **kıyıdan:** from the shore (ablative)
- **birden:** suddenly
- **durdu:** he stopped
- **uzaktaydı:** he was far
- **imdat:** help (interjection)
- **biri beni kurtarsın:** someone save me (imperative)
- **yakınlarda:** nearby (locative)
- **balıkçı kayığında:** in fishing boat (locative)
- **bağırışlarını:** his screams (accusative)
- **oraya:** there (dative)

- **çektiler:** they pulled
- **verdiler:** they gave
- **üşümüş:** he was cold
- **yorulmuştu:** he was tired
- **başarmıştı:** he had managed
- **gözleri:** his eyes
- **bayıldı:** he fainted
- **açtığında:** when he opened
- **kenarında:** on the edge of (locative)
- **ölebilirdin:** you could have died
- **istedim:** I wanted
- **sahipsin:** you have
- **sevmiyorsun:** you don't love
- **neden:** why
- **tabii ki:** of course
- **biliyorsun:** you know
- **yalnızca:** just, only
- **paramı:** my money (accusative)
- **parasını veren:** who pays for
- **hayır:** no (interjection)
- **çünkü:** because
- **eşinim:** I'm your wife
- **güzel görünmek:** to look good/pretty (infinitive)

- **eskisi gibi:** as before
- **bu yüzden:** that's why, therefore
- **bütün:** all
- **içinde:** in (locative)
- **genç:** young
- **bunu:** that (accusative)
- **söylemedin:** you didn't tell
- **bilmiyorum:** I don't know

Questions about the story

1. Oktay, çok para kazanması gerektiğini düşünür çünkü...

   a) Ödemesi gereken borçları vardır.
   b) Yeni bir ev alacaklardır.
   c) Çocukları yeni oyuncaklar ister.
   d) Eşi, ona yeni kıyafetler almasını ister.

2. Oktay, eşinin artık onu sevmediğini düşünür. Doğru mu, yanlış mı?

   a) Doğru.
   b) Yanlış.

3. Oktay hangi ölüm yöntemini seçer?

   a) Zehir.
   b) Boğulma.
   c) Yüksekten düşme.
   d) Trafik kazası.

4. Oktay'ı boğulmaktan cankurtaran kurtarır. Doğru mu, yanlış mı?

   a) Doğru.
   b) Yanlış.

5. Eşi, yeni kıyafetler ister çünkü ...

   a) Kıyafetlerini bir kereden fazla giymez.
   b) Kirlileri yıkayacak çamaşır makineleri yoktur.
   c) Kocasına güzel görünmek ister.
   d) Yeni kıyafetleriyle gösteriş yapmak ister.

Answers

1) D – His wife wants him to buy new clothes for her.
2) A – True.
3) B – Drowning.
4) B – False.
5) C – She wants to look beautiful for her husband.

Chapter VII

ÖN YARGI — THE PREJUDİCE

Ankara'ya doğru **yola çıkmıştım**. Birkaç saat içinde **çocuklarıma** ve **eşime kavuşacaktım**. Bunun heyecanıyla arabamın **gaz pedalına** daha sert **bastım**. Bir an önce evime **varmak** istiyordum.

Bir **kavşakta kırmızı ışığı** son anda **fark ederek** arabamı **yavaşlattım**. Yeşil ışığın yanmasını sabırsızlıkla **bekliyordum** ki birden **sarsıldım**. **Emniyet kemerim** olmasa **muhtemelen** başımı ön cama veya **direksiyona** vuracaktım. **Ne olduğunu** anlamaya **çalışırken** biraz önce yanımdan hızla **geçen** aracın **camlarının paramparça** olduğunu ve **yolun kenarına** doğru savrulduğunu gördüm. Kemerimi **çözdüm**, arabadan **indim**.

Arabama baktığımda **şok oldum, ellerim** birden **buz gibi oldu**. İki ay önce aldığım **yepyeni** otomobilimin **farları** kırılmış, tamponu **çizilmiş**, sağ kapı içeri **göçmüştü**. Kafamı **kaldırdığımda** bana **vuran şoför**ün hızla kaçtığını **fark ettim**. Öfkeyle yeniden **direksiyona geçtim**.

Birkaç **dakika** içinde bana vuran arabaya **yetiştim** ve arabamdan **hızlıca** çıkıp şoförün yanına gittim. Çok **öfkeliydim**.

— **Ne yaptığını sanıyorsun? Utanmaz** adam! diye bağırdım.
— **Beyefendi**, neler söylüyorsunuz? Bu kadar öfkelenecek **ne var?** **Alt tarafı** küçük bir **çizik...**

"**Küçük** bir çizik mi? Bu adam benimle **dalga geçiyor**." diye düşünürken **kafamı** otobilime **çevirdim**. Ezilen **kapıyı**, kırılan farları

60

aradım **fakat** her şey **sapasağlamdı.** Yalnızca adamın **dediği gibi** ufak biz çizik **vardı.** Adam **önce** arabama, **sonra** yüzüme **baktı.**

— Sanırım biraz **abarttınız.** Arabanıza vurduğumu **kabul ediyorum,** bunun için **özür dilerim,** dedi.

Aileme kavuşmanın **heyecanıyla** o gece hiç **uyumamıştım. Saatlerdir** araba **kullanıyordum** ve çok yorgundum. Bu yüzden **zihnim** ufak bir çiziği **korkunç** bir **çarpışma** olarak **algılamıştı. Nasıl cevap vereceğimi** düşünüyordum.

— Arabanıza vurdum ama **o kadar çaresizdim** ki! dedi adam.

— Anlamadım?

— **Benimle gelin** lütfen.

Birlikte onun **otomobiline** doğru yürüdük. Kapıyı açtığında **kucağında** yedi sekiz **yaşlarında** bir çocuk olan **kadını** gördüm. **Ağlıyordu.**

— **Kızım** çok **hasta.** Onu **hastaneye** götürmem gerekiyordu. **Anlıyor musunuz?** dedi adam.

Adamın bu **sözlerine nasıl** cevap vereceğimi **bilmiyordum.** Çok **utanmıştım. Başımı eğdim** ve arabama doğru yürümeye **başladım. Birkaç adım** sonra adam koşarak yanıma geldi.

— Bir dakika, **bekleyin!** Adresim ve **telefonum** bu kartta **yazılı. Beni** lütfen **arayın. Zararınız** neyse **ödeyeceğim,** dedi.

— Peki.

— Sizden **kaçmayı** düşünmedim. Size vurduktan sonra **plakanızı not aldım.** Siz beni **durdurmasaydınız** kızımı hastaneye götürdükten sonra size **ulaşacaktım,** dedi adam.

O **konuştukça** ben **daha fazla** utanıyordum. Tam **bir şey daha** söylemek **üzereydi** ki onun konuşmasına **fırsat** vermeden **bağırdım.**

— **Yeter!** Hadi, bin arabana, kızını hastaneye **götür!** Hadi, **durma!**

Ne olduğunu, neden bağırdığımı **anlayamadı. Ardından** arabasına **döndü** ve birkaç saniye **içerisinde gözden kayboldu.**

Yol boyunca başıma gelen bu **olayı** düşündüm. Nasıl **olmuştu** bu? Arabamda büyük bir **hasar** gördüğüme **emindim. Beynimiz** nasıl böyle oyunlar **oynuyordu** bize?

Yaşadığım bu olayın beni çok **daha ciddi** bir **kaza**dan **koruduğuna** inanıyorum **şimdi.** O gün **o olay** olmasaydı **yorgun zihnim belki** de büyük bir **hata** yapmama **yol açacaktı.** Adamın bana verdiği **kartı** hâlâ **saklıyorum.** Onu **hiç** aramadım. **Umarım** çocuğu **iyileşmiştir.** Belki **bir gün,** bir yerde **karşılaşırız.**

Hikayenin Özeti

Bu hikayede anlatıcı, yaptığı yolculuklardan birinde yaşadıklarını anlatır. Evine dönerken kaza yapar ve aracına vuran şoför durmadan kaçar. Bunun üzerine anlatıcı, ona çarpan aracın peşinden gider ve şoförü yakalayıp onunla tartışmaya başlar. Fakat şoförün hasta bir kızı olduğunu ve onu hastaneye götürmek için acele etmek zorunda kaldığını öğrenir. Şoför iyi bir adamdır ve niyeti vurup kaçmak değildir. Hatta hasarı daha sonra karşılamak için vurduğu aracın plakasını bile almıştır. Anlatıcı, adamı dinlemeden yargıladığı için pişman olur, utanır ve ona bir an önce kızını hastaneye götürmesini söyler.

Summary of the story

In this story, the narrator tells what he has experienced on one of his journeys. On his way home, he has an accident and the driver who hit his car flees from the scene instead of stopping. Then the narrator chases the car, catches the driver and starts to argue with him. He finds out that the driver's daughter is sick and he has to hurry to take her to the hospital. He is a good man and his intention is not "hit and run". He has even taken down the plate number of the vehicle so that he can cover the damage later. The narrator regrets and feels ashamed that he has judged him without listening and tells him to take his daughter to the hospital as soon as possible.

Vocabulary

- **yola çıkmıştım:** I have set off
- **çocuklarıma:** my kids (dative)
- **eşime:** my wife (dative)
- **kavuşacaktım:** I was going to reunite with
- **gaz pedalına:** gas pedal (dative)
- **bastım:** I pushed
- **varmak:** to arrive (infinitive)
- **kavşakta:** at crossroad (locative)
- **kırmızı:** red
- **ışığı:** light (accusative)
- **fark ederek:** noticing (adverb)
- **yavaşlattım:** I slowed down
- **bekliyordum:** I was waiting
- **sarsıldım:** I was shaken
- **emniyet kemerim:** my seat belt
- **muhtemelen:** probably
- **direksiyona:** wheel (dative)
- **ne olduğunu:** what happened (accusative)
- **çalışırken:** while trying to
- **geçen:** passing (adjective)
- **camlar:** windows
- **paramparça:** shattered
- **yolun kenarına:** side of the road (dative)
- **çözdüm:** I unfastened
- **indim:** I got out
- **arabama:** my car (dative)
- **şok oldum:** I got shocked
- **ellerim:** my hands
- **buz gibi oldu:** they went cold
- **iki:** two
- **ay:** month
- **yepyeni:** brand new
- **farları:** headlights of (possessive)
- **çizilmiş:** it was scratched
- **göçmüştü:** it caved in
- **kaldırdığımda:** when I raised
- **vuran:** who hit
- **şoför:** driver
- **fark ettim:** I realized
- **direksiyona geçtim:** I took the wheel
- **dakika:** minute
- **yetiştim:** I caught/reached

- **hızlıca:** quickly
- **öfkeliydim:** I was pissed off
- **ne yaptığını sanıyorsun:** what do you think you are doing
- **utanmaz:** shameless
- **beyefendi:** sir
- **ne var:** what's so
- **alt tarafı:** just, only, after all
- **çizik:** scratch
- **küçük:** tiny
- **dalga geçiyor:** he is kidding
- **kafamı:** my head (accusative)
- **çevirdim:** I turned
- **kapıyı:** the door (accusative)
- **kırılan:** broken (adjective)
- **fakat:** but
- **sapasağlamdı:** it was fine
- **dediği gibi:** as he said
- **vardı:** there was
- **önce:** first
- **sonra:** then
- **baktı:** he looked
- **abarttınız:** you exaggerated
- **kabul ediyorum:** I admit
- **özür dilerim:** I'm sorry
- **aileme:** my family (dative)
- **heyecanıyla:** with the excitement
- **uyumamıştım:** I hadn't sleep
- **saatlerdir:** for hours
- **kullanıyordum:** I had been driving
- **zihnim:** my mind
- **korkunç:** terrible
- **çarpışma:** crash
- **algılamıştı:** it perceived
- **nasıl cevap vereceğimi:** how I will answer (accusative)
- **kadar:** so
- **çaresizdim:** I was desperate
- **benimle:** with me
- **gelin:** you come (imperative, plural/formal)
- **birlikte:** together
- **otomobiline:** his car (dative)
- **kucağında:** on her lap (locative)
- **yaşlarında:** years old
- **kadını:** the woman (accusative)
- **ağlıyordu:** she was crying
- **kızım:** my daughter
- **hasta:** sick

- **hastaneye:** to hospital (dative)
- **anlıyor musunuz:** do you understand
- **sözlerine:** his words (dative)
- **nasıl:** how
- **bilmiyordum:** I didn't know
- **utanmıştım:** I was embarrased
- **başımı eğdim:** I hanged my head [in shame]
- **başladım:** I started
- **birkaç:** a few
- **adım:** step
- **bekleyin:** you wait (imperative, plural/formal)
- **telefonum:** my phone number
- **yazılı:** it is written
- **beni arayın:** you call me (imperative, plural/formal)
- **zararınız:** your damages (plural/formal)
- **ödeyeceğim:** I will pay
- **kaçmayı:** to run away (accusative)
- **plakanızı:** your license plate (accusative)
- **not aldım:** I took note
- **durdurmasaydınız:** if you hadn't stopped me
- **ulaşacaktım:** I was going to reach you
- **konuştukça:** as he spoke
- **daha fazla:** more
- **bir şey daha:** one more thing
- **üzereydi:** he was about
- **fırsat:** opportunity
- **bağırdım:** I shouted
- **yeter:** that is enough
- **hadi:** come on (interjection)
- **götür:** you take (imperative)
- **durma:** don't stop (imperative)
- **anlayamadı:** he couldn't understand
- **ardından:** then, afterwards
- **döndü:** he returned
- **içerisinde:** in [in seconds]
- **gözden kayboldu:** he dissappeared
- **yol boyunca:** along the way
- **olayı:** the incident (accusative)
- **olmuştu:** it has happened
- **hasar:** damage
- **emindim:** I was sure

- **beynimiz:** our brain
- **oynuyordu:** it was playing
- **daha ciddi:** more serious
- **kaza:** accident
- **koruduğuna:** that it protected (dative)
- **şimdi:** now
- **olay:** that incident
- **yorgun:** tired
- **zihnim:** my mind
- **belki:** maybe
- **hata:** mistake
- **yol açacaktı:** it would have caused
- **kartı:** the card (accusative)
- **saklıyorum:** I keep
- **hiç:** never
- **umarım:** I hope
- **iyileşmiştir:** she has recovered
- **bir gün:** someday
- **karşılaşırız:** we will meet

Questions about the story

1. **Anlatıcı kendisini neden yorgun hissediyordur?**

   a) Saatlerdir araba kullanıyordur.
   b) Zihni düşüncelerle doludur.
   c) Yatıştırıcı ilaç almıştır.
   d) Hastadır.

2. **Anlatıcı, kafasını direksiyona çarpar. Doğru mu, yanlış mı?**

   a) Doğru.
   b) Yanlış.

3. **Adam neden telefon numarasını ve adresini verir?**

   a) Anlatıcıyla arkadaş olmak ister.
   b) Hasarı karşılamak ister.
   c) Anlatıcıyı partiye çağırmak ister.
   d) Anlatıcıdan sabıka kayıtlarını kontrol etmesini ister.

4. **Anlatıcının arabası kötü şekilde hasara uğramıştır. Doğru mu, yanlış mı?**

   a) Doğru.
   b) Yanlış.

5. **Adam arabasının kapısını açtığında anlatıcı ... görür.**

   a) Mülteciler.
   b) Yaralı bir köpek.
   c) Ağlayan bir kadın ve küçük bir çocuk.
   d) Doğum yapan bir kadın.

Answers

1) A – He has been driving for hours.
2) B – False.
3) B – He wants to compensate for the damage.
4) B – False.
5) C – A crying woman and a little kid.

Chapter VIII

GÜNEŞ VE AY — THE SUN AND THE MOON

Osmanlı Sultanı **Muhteşem** Süleyman'ın **kızı**, 17 yaşına **basmıştı**. Bu kızın ismi, **Farsçada** "**güneş** ve **ay**" anlamına gelen Mihrimah'tı. **Evlilik** yaşına geldiği için uygun bir **taliple** evlenecekti. Taliplerden biri, Osmanlı **İmparatorluğu'nun** en zengin **valilerinden** biriydi. Mihrimah Sultan'ın evlilikle **ilgili** herhangi bir **fikir** belirtme **hakkı yoktu**. O, hakkında **verilen kararlara uymak** zorundaydı. **Böylece** Mihrimah'ın vali ile evlenmesine **karar verildi**.

Bu evlilik kararı, imparatorluğun "**başmimarı**" olan Mimar Sinan için **ne yazık ki üzücü** bir **haber**di. Mimar Sinan, yaptığı **görkemli** eserlerle **tanınmış** olan çok **ünlü** bir **mimardı**. Sinan, Mihrimah'a çok **aşıktı**; fakat ne yazık ki Mimar Sinan 50 yaşındaydı ve **evliydi**. **Bu nedenle** Mihrimah Sultan'la **evlenmek için** talip **olması mümkün değildi**. Mimar Sinan, bu haberi **duyunca** çok üzülmesine **rağmen** aşkını **kalbine gömdü** ve kendini işlerine **adadı**.

Mihrimah Sultan, vali **ile** evlendi. Aradan **yıllar** geçti. Annesinin ve kocasının **ölümünün ardından** Mihrimah, sultan olan babasına **yardım etmeye** başladı. Ona **tavsiyeler** veren **akıl hocası** olma görevini üstlendi. **Hayatı boyunca** birçok **devlet işinde söz sahibi oldu**.

Derken bir gün, Mimar Sinan **saraya** çağrıldı ve kendisine yeni bir **görev verildi**. Ondan İstanbul'un iki **girişine** Mihrimah Sultan'ın **adını**

taşıyan birer **cami** yapması istenmişti. **Bunlardan** biri Üsküdar'da, diğeri ise Edirnekapı'da **olacaktı.**

Mimar Sinan işe **başladı. Her zamanki gibi** yaptığı işe çok önem veriyor, **detaylar** üzerinde **özenle** çalışıyordu. Sinan, her zaman detaylara önem verirdi. Ancak **bu sefer yarattığı** bu iki **eser**deki detaylarda **sanki** bir şeyler **gizliydi.** Camilerden biri, **eteği** yerleri **süpüren** bir **kadın silüetine benziyordu.** Diğer caminin **avizelerinde** ise **upuzun** saçları olan bir kadının **görüntüsü** bulunuyordu. Mimar Sinan, Mihrimah'a olan **aşkını** bu camilerle **yansıtmıştı.** O büyük bir **sanatçıydı.** Yıllardan beri **yüreğinde sakladığı duygular,** Mihrimah Sultan için yaptığı bu iki esere **yansımıştı.**

Fakat **ilginç** olan **sadece** bu değildi. **Her iki** cami de **Güneş'in doğuşu** ve batışı **hesap edilerek** yapılmıştı. 21 Mart'ta, bir caminin **arkasından** Güneş **batarken diğer** caminin arkasından Ay **yükseliyordu.** Güneş ve ay; **yani** Mihrimah isminin **anlamı...** Camiler, **İstanbul'a** Mihrimah'ın **adını fısıldıyor** gibiydi.

Peki, Sinan **niçin** Güneş'in ve Ay'ın 21 Mart'taki **konumunu** düşünerek **çizmişti** camilerin **planlarını?** 21 Mart, Mihrimah Sultan'ın **doğum günüydü. Yılda bir kez,** Mihrimah Sultan'ın doğum gününde, Güneş ve Ay **camilerin üzerinde buluşuyordu.** Sinan, Güneş'in ve Ay'ın birbirleriyle buluşmasını **sağlayabilmişti** ama **kendisi** Mihrimah Sultan ile **asla** buluşamamıştı.

Bu **öykü** yıllar boyunca **anlatıldı** ve **günümüze dek** ulaştı. **Bazıları** bunun sadece bir **söylenti** olduğunu, **Sinan'ın aşkı** ile ilgili bir **kanıt** bulunmadığını söyledi. **İnsanların çoğu** ise bu öykünün **gerçek** olduğuna **inandı. Ya siz?**

Hikayenin Özeti

Bu, Osmanlı İmparatorluğu'nun tarihinden bir aşk hikayesidir. Kanuni Sultan Süleyman'ın kızı evlenecektir. Onun adı "güneş ve ay" anlamına gelen Mihrimah'tır. Sarayın başmimarı Sinan, ona çok aşıktır ama yaşlı bir adamdır ve zaten evlidir. Dolayısıyla Mihrimah başka biriyle evlenir.

Ardından Sinan, İstanbul'un girişlerine iki cami inşa etmek için görevlendirilir ve kalbini mimarisine döker. 21 Mart'ta, camilerden birinin arkasında Güneş batarken diğerinden Ay yükselir. Mihrimah isminin anlamı; güneş ve aydır. 21 Mart Mihrimah'ın doğum günüdür.

Summary of the story

This is a love story from the history of the Ottoman Empire. The daughter of Suleiman the Magnificent will get married. Her name is Mihrimah, which means the sun and the moon. The chief architect of the palace, Sinan, is deeply in love with her but he is and old man and married already. So, Mihrimah gets married with someone else.

Thereafter, Sinan has been commissioned to build mosques at the entrances of İstanbul and he pours his heart into his architecture. On March 21, the sun sets behind one of the mosques while the moon comes out behind the other one. The sun and the moon: the meaning of Mihrimah's name. March 21 is Mihrimah's birthday.

Vocabulary

- **Osmanlı:** Ottoman
- **muhteşem:** magnificent
- **kızı:** his daughter
- **basmıştı:** she had turned
- **Farsçada:** in Persian (locative)
- **güneş:** the sun
- **ay:** the moon
- **evlilik:** marriage
- **talip:** suitor
- **imparatorluğunun:** of Empire's (possessive)
- **valililer:** governors
- **ilgili:** about
- **fikir:** opinion
- **hakkı yoktu:** she didn't have right
- **verilen:** which was made
- **kararlara:** decisions (dative)
- **uymak:** to obey, to abide by (infinitive)
- **böylece:** so
- **karar verildi:** decision was made
- **başmimar:** chief architect
- **ne yazık ki:** unfortunately
- **üzücü:** sad
- **haber:** news
- **görkemli:** magnificent, gorgeous
- **tanınmış:** known
- **ünlü:** famous
- **mimardı:** he was architect (past tense)
- **aşıktı:** he was in love
- **evliydi:** he was married
- **bu nedenle:** for that reason
- **evlenmek için:** in order to marry
- **olması:** to be (possessive)
- **mümkün değildi:** it was not possible
- **duyunca:** when he heard
- **rağmen:** even though
- **kalbine:** his heart (dative)
- **gömdü:** he buried

- **adadı:** he dedicated
- **ile:** with
- **yıllar:** years
- **ölümünün:** of the death of (possessive)
- **ardından:** after
- **yardım etmeye:** to help (dative)
- **tavsiyeler:** advices
- **akıl hocası:** advisor
- **hayatı boyunca:** throughout her life
- **devlet işi:** state affair
- **söz sahibi oldu:** she had a say
- **derken:** then, meanwhile
- **saraya:** to palace
- **görev verildi:** she was commissioned
- **girişine:** at the entrance (dative)
- **adını taşıyan:** that bear her name
- **cami:** mosque
- **bunlardan:** of them
- **olacaktı:** it would be
- **başladı:** he started
- **her zamanki gibi:** as always
- **detaylar:** details
- **özenle:** diligently
- **bu sefer:** this time
- **yarattığı:** that he created
- **eser:** artwork
- **sanki:** seems like, as if
- **gizliydi:** it was hidden
- **eteği:** her skirt
- **süpüren:** sweeping (adjective)
- **kadın:** woman
- **silüetine:** silhouette of (dative)
- **benziyordu:** it was resembling
- **avizelerinde:** in chandeliers (locative)
- **upuzun:** very long
- **görüntüsü:** the image of
- **aşkını:** his love (accusative)
- **yansıtmıştı:** he reflected
- **sanatçıydı:** he was artist
- **yüreğinde:** in his heart (locative)
- **sakladığı:** that he treasured
- **duygular:** emotions
- **yansımıştı:** it was reflected
- **ilginç:** interesting

- **sadece:** only
- **her iki:** both
- **güneşin doğuşu:** sunrise
- **hesap edilerek:** by calculating
- **arkasından:** from behind (ablative)
- **batarken:** while [the sun] was setting
- **diğer:** other
- **yükseliyordu:** it was coming out
- **yani:** in other words, so
- **anlamı:** meaning of
- **İstanbul'a:** to İstanbul (dative)
- **adını:** her name (accusative)
- **fısıldıyor:** it is whispering
- **peki:** so
- **niçin:** why
- **konumunu:** the location of (accusative)
- **çizmişti:** he drew
- **planlarını:** the plans (accusative)
- **doğum günüydü:** it was her birthday
- **yılda bir kez:** once a year
- **camilerin üzerinde:** over the mosques
- **buluşuyordu:** they were coming together
- **sağlayabilmişti:** he could manage
- **kendisi:** himself
- **asla:** never
- **öykü:** story
- **anlatıldı:** it was told
- **günümüze dek:** until today
- **bazıları:** some of them
- **söylenti:** rumor
- **Sinan'ın aşkı:** Sinan's love
- **kanıt:** proof
- **insanların çoğu:** most of the people
- **gerçek:** true
- **inandı:** he/she believed
- **ya siz:** what about you

Questions about the story

1. **Hangi dilde Mihrimah 'güneş ve ay' anlamına gelir?**

   a) Türkçe.

   b) Arapça.

   c) Farsça.

   d) Osmanlıca.

2. **Mihrimah, Mimar Sinan'la evlenir. Doğru mu, yanlış mı?**

   a) Doğru.

   b) Yanlış.

3. **Sinan, evlilik için uygun bir talip değildi çünkü ...**

   a) İşleriyle çok meşguldür.

   b) Yaşlı ve evlidir.

   c) Padişah onu sevmez.

   d) Başka bir kadına aşıktır.

4. **21 Mart'ı Sinan için önemli kılan nedir?**

   a) Kanuni Sultan Süleyman'ın öldüğü gündür.

   b) Mihrimah'ın öldüğü gündür.

   c) Mihrimah'ın evlendiği gündür.

   d) Mihrimah'ın doğduğu gündür.

5. **Bu aşk hikayesinin gerçekliğine dair bir kanıt yoktur. Doğru mu, yanlış mı?**

   a) Doğru.

   b) Yanlış.

Answers

1) C – Persian.
2) B – False.
3) B – He is old and married.
4) D – It's the day when Mihrimah was born.
5) A – True.

Chapter IX

MERHAMET — THE MERCY

Kumar tutkum **sebebiyle** geçmişte birçok ülkeyi **ziyaret ettim.** Gittiğim yerlerde zengin **iş adamlarıyla** tanışır, bazılarıyla **arkadaş** olurdum. Akın da **bunlardan biriydi. Babasının** Türkiye'de büyük bir **yat firması** vardı. O ise **Kıbrıs'ta** bir **kumarhane işletiyordu.**

Kıbrıs'ta **bulunduğum** günlerden birinde **beni aradı** ve ofisine **davet etti. Konu** paraya **gelince** ona kumarhanenin **karşılıksız çekler**den dolayı **ne kadar** para **kaybettiğini** sordum.

— **Birkaç** hafta önce ilginç bir **deneyim** yaşadım, sana **anlatayım,** dedi.

Akın **konuşmayı** pek sevmezdi ama **bu defa** benim konuşmama **fırsat vermeden** anlatmaya başladı:

— Bir gün **çalışanlarımdan biri,** bir kadının benimle **konuşmak** istediğini ve **isminin** Emine Kızıltepe olduğunu **söyledi.** Saim Kızıltepe'yi **tanıdığım** için **eşiyle** görüşmeyi **kabul ettim.** Kadın **içeri** girer girmez **ağlamaya** başladı. **Gözyaşlarını mendille** silmeye çalışıyordu. Normalde **bu tür şeyleri** sevmem ama **bu durum** beni çok **etkiledi.** Geçen gün kocasının **buraya** geldiğini ve **çok para** kaybettiğini söyledi. Ben Saim Bey'i **tanıyorum. Her yıl** belli zamanlarda buraya **gelir.**

— Yani arkadaşın, öyle mi? diye sordum.

— Hayır. Onu **yıllardır** burada görüyordum ama ne kazanıp ne kaybettiği hakkında bir **fikrim yoktu.** Emine Hanım da kocasına kumar oynamaması için **yalvardığını** ama adamın onu **dinlemediğini** söyledi. Geçen gün Saim Bey'in para kaybetmesi de onların **hayatını mahvetmiş**. Evlerini **satmışlar**. İki **kızları** varmış ve **okuldan** almak **zorunda** kalmışlar. Bu durum beni çok etkiledi. **Aynı zamanda** kumarhanemin **bu tip** bir **şöhret** kazanmasını da istemedim. Kadına kocasının kaybettiği parayı **geri vermeyi** bir **şartla** kabul ettim. Kocasının **bir daha** kumarhaneme **gelmemesini** istedim. Parası **yoksa oynamamalı**. Emine Hanım da bana **teşekkür etti** ve bu konuda **söz verdi**.

— Kadın için **üzüldüm**, diye yanıtladım.

— **Dahası var**, dedi. **Ertesi gün,** Saim Bey'i masalardan birinde **kumar oynarken** gördüm. Çok **sinirlendim**. Yanına gidip 'Bir dakika **konuşabilir miyiz?**' dedim.

— Tabii ki, dedi.

— Konuşmak için **kalabalıktan** uzak bir **köşeye** gittik. "Buraya gelerek **ne yapmaya çalışıyorsunuz?**" diye sordum. **Amacının** ne olduğunu **anlayamamıştım**. Eşinin beni **görmeye geldiğini**, **kaybettiği parayı** bana anlattığını söyledim. **Ayrıca** onun bir daha **buraya** gelmemesi şartıyla eşine **tüm parayı** geri verdiğimi de **ekledim**. Adam **bir süre** yüzüme baktı. "Sanırım bir **hata** olmuş, ben **evli değilim** ki!" dedi.

Hikayenin Özeti

Akın, zengin bir iş adamının oğludur ve Kıbrıs'ta bir kumarhane işletmektedir. Bir gün kumarhanesine bir kadın gelir ve kocasının kumar yüzünden çok para kaybettiğini söyler. Evlerini satmak ve çocuklarını okuldan almak zorunda kaldıklarını da ekler. Akın bu duruma üzülür. Kadına kocası bir daha kumarhaneye gelmezse ona kaybettiği parayı geri vereceğini söyler. Bunun üzerine kadın söz verir, parayı alır ve gider. Ertesi gün Akın adamı kumarhanesinde görür. Neden geldiğini ona sormak için yanına yaklaştığında acı gerçeği öğrenir; adam evli değildir.

Summary of the story

Akın is the son of a wealthy businessman and runs a casino in Cyprus. One day, a woman comes to his casino and tells him that her husband has lost a lot of money because of gambling. She also adds that they had to sell their home and take their children out of school. Akın feels sorry about this situation. He tells the woman that he will give her the money back if her husband doesn't come to his casino again. Then the woman promises, takes the money and leaves. The next day, Akın sees the man in his casino. When he approaches him to ask him why he came, he finds out the sad truth: the man is not married.

Vocabulary

- **kumar:** gambling
- **sebebiyle:** due to, because of
- **ziyaret ettim:** I had traveled
- **iş adamları:** businessmen
- **arkadaş:** friend
- **bunlardan biriydi:** he was one of them (past tense)
- **babasının:** his father's (possessive)
- **yat firması:** yatch company
- **Kıbrıs'ta:** in Cyprus (locative)
- **kumarhane:** casino
- **işletiyordu:** he was running
- **bulunduğum:** when/that I was in
- **beni:** me (accusative)
- **aradı:** he called
- **davet etti:** he invited
- **konu … gelince:** when it comes to …
- **karşılıksız çekler:** bad checks
- **ne kadar:** how much
- **kaybettiğini:** that he lost (accusative)
- **birkaç:** a few
- **deneyim:** experience
- **anlatayım:** let me tell (optative)
- **konuşmayı:** talking (accusative)
- **bu defa:** this time
- **fırsat vermeden:** without giving chance
- **çalışanlarımdan biri:** one of my employees
- **konuşmak:** to talk (infinitive)
- **isminin:** her name's (possessive)
- **söyledi:** she said
- **tanıdığım:** that I know
- **eşiyle:** with his wife
- **kabul ettim:** I accepted
- **içeri:** inside
- **ağlamaya:** crying (dative)
- **gözyaşlarını:** her tears (accusative)
- **mendille:** with handkerchief
- **bu tür şeyleri:** that sort of things (accusative)
- **bu durum:** this situation

- **etkiledi:** it impressed
- **buraya:** here (dative)
- **çok:** so much
- **para:** money
- **tanıyorum:** I know
- **her yıl:** every year
- **gelir:** he comes
- **yıllardır:** for years
- **fikrim yoktu:** I had no idea
- **yalvardığını:** that she begged (accusative)
- **dinlemediğini:** that he didn't listen
- **hayatını:** their life (accusative)
- **mahvetmiş:** it ruined
- **satmışlar:** they had sold
- **kızları:** their daughters
- **okuldan:** out of school (ablative)
- **zorunda:** have to
- **aynı zamanda:** at the same time
- **bu tip:** that kind of
- **şöhret:** reputation
- **geri vermeyi:** to give back
- **şartla:** on one condition
- **bir daha:** again
- **gelmemesini:** that he shouldn't come (accusative)
- **yoksa:** otherwise
- **oynamamalı:** he shouldn't play
- **teşekkür etti:** she thanked
- **söz verdi:** she promised
- **üzüldüm:** I felt sad
- **dahası var:** there is more
- **ertesi gün:** the next day
- **kumar oynarken:** while gambling
- **sinirlendim:** I got mad
- **konuşabilir miyiz:** can we talk
- **kalabalıktan:** from the crowd (ablative)
- **köşeye:** to corner (dative)
- **ne yapmaya çalışıyorsunuz:** what are you trying to do
- **amacının:** his purpose's (possessive)
- **anlayamamıştım:** I couldn't understand
- **görmeye geldiğini:** that she came to see (accusative)
- **kaybettiği parayı:** the money he lost (accusative)
- **ayrıca:** besides, also
- **buraya:** here (dative)
- **tüm parayı:** all the money (accusative)

- **ekledim:** I added
- **bir süre:** for a while
- **hata:** mistake

- **evli değilim:** I am not married

Questions about the story

1. **Akın, Kıbrıs'ta bir ... işletiyordur.**

   a) Yat firması.

   b) Tersane.

   c) Kumarhane.

   d) İnternet kafe.

2. **Akın, konuşmayı pek sevmez. Doğru mu, yanlış mı?**

   a) Doğru.

   b) Yanlış.

3. **Emine Kızıltepe, ... Akın'la görüşmek ister.**

   a) Onu işe almasını istemek için.

   b) Kocasının para kaybettiğini söylemek için.

   c) İşletmeye ortak olmak için.

   d) Yat şirketleri hakkında bilgi almak için.

4. **Kadının kocası kumarhanaeye bir daha gelmez. Doğru mu, yanlış mı?**

   a) Doğru.

   b) Yanlış.

5. **Akın, adamla konuşunca ... öğrenir.**

   a) Adamın zengin olduğunu.

   b) Adamın evli olmadığını.

   c) Adamın Türk olmadığını.

   d) Adamın kumar oynamadığını.

Answers

1) C – Casino.
2) A – True.
3) B – To tell him that his husband has lost money.
4) B – False.
5) B – That the man is not married.

Chapter X

DOĞUM GÜNÜ — BİRTHDAY

Cemile, **bir sabah** aniden **hayatımıza** girdi. Üzerinde **eski püskü** giysiler, **ayaklarında yırtık** bir **çift ayakkabı** vardı. Cemile, Adana'ya **mevsimlik** göçmen olarak gelen **işçiler**den birinin **kızıydı**. Bu işçiler o kadar **yoksullardı** ki kazandıkları para ailelerini **geçindirmeye** bile **yetmiyordu.**

Öğretmenimiz yoklama defterine Cemile'nin adını yazarken Cemile, **sınıfın ortasında dikilmiş,** ellerini **ceplerinde saklıyordu.** Sınıfa yeni gelen bu **zavallı görünümlü** arkadaşımıza karşı nasıl **davranmamız** gerektiğini **bilmiyorduk. Arka sıradaki** öğrenciler **fısıldaşıyordu.** Arkamda **oturan** çocuk:

— **Bu ne?** diye fısıldadı yanındakine.

— Biriniz **pencereyi açın,** dedi öteki.

Öğretmenimiz **gözlüklerinin** üzerinden **bize baktı** ve tüm sınıf bir anda **sustu.**

— Evet, bu yeni **arkadaşınız** Cemile, dedi.

Cemile, sınıfa şöyle bir **bakındı** ve **gülümsedi.** Bizim de ona gülümsememizi **bekliyordu.** Fakat **tüm sınıf** gözlerini ona dikmişti, kimse hiçbir **tepki** vermiyordu. O ise **hâlâ** gülümsemeye **devam ediyordu.**

Nefesimi tutmuş öğretmenimizin yanımdaki **boş** sırayı **fark etmemesi** için **dua ediyordum** ama fark etti. Cemile'ye **parmağıyla** o sırayı **işaret etti.** Sırasına **otururken** gözlerime baktı **ama arkadaş** olabileceğimize dair ona **umut** vermemek için **kafamı çevirdim.**

İlk **haft**anın **sonunda** Cemile, kendine arkadaş **bulamamıştı**. Bir akşam yemekte anneme:

— Bu **onun hatası**. Daha **sayı saymayı** bile bilmiyor, dedim.

Cemile **hakkındaki** yorumlarım**dan dolayı** annem onu tanıyordu artık.

Cemile elinde **yemek tepsisi**, **yüzünde** gülümsemeyle önümde durdu.

— **Yanına** oturabilir miyim? dedi.

Birinin bizi görüp görmediğini anlamak için **etrafa göz attım**.

— **Peki**, dedim.

Onun yemeğini yemesini **izlerken** Cemile hakkındaki **yorumlarımız**da pek **haklı** olmadığımızı anladım. **İyi** bir kızdı, **tanıdığım** en **neşeli** kızlardan biriydi. Yemeği bitirdikten **sonra** sınıfa **girerken** onunla arkadaş olmaya **karar vermiştim**.

Bir **gece** onu **düşünürken** annem **odama** geldi.

— Anne, sence **çocuklar** neden Cemile'ye bu kadar **kötü davranıyorlar**? diye sordum.

— **Bilmiyorum**, belki de **tek** bildikleri şey **budur**, diye yanıtladı.

— **Yarın** onun **doğum günü**. Kimse ona **hediye** vermeyecek. **Pastası** olmayacak. Kimsenin **umurunda değil**.

Birinin doğum günü **olduğunda** pasta **yenir**, sınıfta **kutlanırdı**. İkimiz de bunu biliyorduk. Cemile'nin **ailesi tarlada** çalışıyordu. Kimse ona pasta **getirmeyecekti**.

— **Üzülme**, **belki** her şey **çok güzel** olur, dedi annem.

Ertesi sabah ilk iş olarak Cemile'nin doğum gününü **kutladım**. Fakat **benim dışımda** bunu umursayan kimse **yoktu**. Belki onun da hiçbir **beklentisi** yoktu. Günün **ilerleyen saatlerinde** ben de doğum günlerinin o kadar **önemli** olmadığını **düşünmeye** başlamıştım.

Ders **sırasında** çok **tanıdık** bir ses **işittim**. Hemen **ardından** sınıfın kapısı açıldı ve annem **elinde** kocaman bir **doğum günü pastası** ve **mumlarla içeriye** girdi. **Kolunun** altında **hediye paketi**ne **sarılmış** küçük bir **kutu** vardı. **Annem** Cemile'yi hemen **tanımış olmalı** ki yüzünü ona çevirerek:

— Cemile, **Doğum günün kutlu olsun!** dedi.

Hikayenin Özeti

Cemile, okulda yenidir. Adana'da mevsimlik işçi olarak çalışan fakir bir aileden gelmektedir. Dış görünüşü yüzünden kimse onunla arkadaş olmak istemez. Fakat anlatıcı, onun için üzülmeye başlar ve onunla arkadaş olmaya karar verir.

Cemile'nin doğum günüdür. Anlatıcı, onun doğum gününü kimsenin kutlamayacağını düşünür çünkü sınıfta kimse onu önemsemez. Doğum günü olduğundan haberleri bile yoktur. Fakat ders sırasında biri sınıfa girer ve ona sürpriz yapar.

Summary of the story

Cemile is new at the school. She comes from a poor family working as seasonal workers in Adana. Nobody wants to be friends with her because of her appearance. However, the narrator starts to feel sorry for her and decides to become friends with her.

It's Cemile's birthday. The narrator thinks that nobody will celebrate it because no one in the class cares about her. They don't even know it's her birthday. However, someone enters the class and makes a surprise for her.

Vocabulary

- **bir sabah:** one morning
- **hayatımıza:** to our lives (dative)
- **eski püskü:** worn out, ragged
- **ayaklarında:** on her feet (locative)
- **yırtık:** torn
- **çift:** pair
- **ayakkabı:** shoe
- **mevsimlik:** seasonal
- **işçiler:** workers
- **kızıydı:** she was the daughter of (past tense)
- **yoksullardı:** they were poor
- **geçindirmeye:** to support [family] (dative)
- **yetmiyordu:** it was not enough
- **öğretmenimiz:** our teacher
- **yoklama:** attendance
- **sınıfın ortasında:** in the middle of class (locative)
- **dikilmiş:** standing (adjective/adverb)
- **ceplerinde:** in her pockets (locative)
- **saklıyordu:** she was hiding
- **zavallı:** poor
- **görünümlü:** looking (adjective)
- **davranmamız:** that we treat
- **bilmiyorduk:** we didn't know
- **arka sıradaki:** that on the back row
- **fısıldaşıyordu:** they were whispering
- **oturan:** sitting (adjective)
- **bu ne:** what's this
- **pencereyi:** window (accusative)
- **açın:** open (imperative, plural/formal)
- **gözlüklerinin:** her glasses' (possessive)
- **bize baktı:** she looked at
- **sustu:** they stopped talking
- **arkadaşınız:** your friend
- **bakındı:** she looked around
- **gülümsedi:** she smiled
- **bekliyordu:** she was waiting

- **tüm sınıf:** whole class (metonym for "everyone in the classroom")
- **tepki:** reaction
- **hâlâ:** still
- **devam ediyordu:** she was continuing to
- **nefesimi:** my breath (accusative)
- **boş:** empy, available, free
- **fark etmemesi:** that she doesn't notice (possessive)
- **dua ediyordum:** I was praying
- **parmağıyla:** with her finger
- **işaret etti:** she pointed out
- **otururken:** while sitting
- **ama:** but
- **arkadaş:** friend
- **umut:** hope
- **kafamı çevirdim:** I turned my head
- **ilk hafta:** first week
- **sonunda:** at the end (locative)
- **bulamamıştı:** she couldn't find
- **onun hatası:** her fault
- **sayı saymayı:** counting (accusative)
- **hakkındaki:** about
- **-dan dolayı:** because of
- **yemek tepsisi:** food tray
- **yüzünde:** on her face (locative)
- **yanına:** next to you
- **birinin:** someone's (possessive)
- **etrafa:** around (accusative)
- **göz attım:** I looked/glanced
- **peki:** alright, well then
- **izlerken:** while watching
- **yorumlarımız:** our thoughts
- **haklı:** right
- **iyi:** good
- **tanıdığım:** that I have met
- **neşeli:** cheerful
- **sonra:** after
- **girerken:** while entering
- **karar vermiştim:** I have decided
- **gece:** night
- **düşünürken:** while thinking
- **odama:** into my room (dative)
- **çocuklar:** kids
- **kötü davranıyorlar:** they are treating bad
- **bilmiyorum:** I don't know
- **tek:** only
- **budur:** that's

- **yarın:** tomorrow
- **doğum günü:** her birthday
- **kimse:** nobody
- **hediye:** present
- **pastası:** her cake
- **umurunda değil:** no one cares
- **olduğunda:** when it's
- **yenir:** it is eaten
- **kutlanırdı:** it is celebrated
- **ikimiz:** both of us
- **ailesi:** her family
- **tarlada:** in the field (locative)
- **getirmeyecekti:** they wouldn't bring
- **üzülme:** don't be sad (imperative)
- **belki:** maybe
- **çok güzel:** great, very good
- **ertesi sabah:** the next morning
- **kutladım:** I celebrated
- **benim dışımda:** except me
- **yoktu:** there wasn't
- **beklentisi:** her expectation
- **ilerleyen saatlerinde:** later in the day (locative)
- **önemli:** important
- **düşünmeye:** to think (dative)
- **sırasında:** during
- **tanıdık:** familiar
- **işittim:** I heard
- **ardından:** then
- **kapısı:** door of (possessive)
- **elinde:** in her hand (locative)
- **doğum günü pastası:** birthday cake
- **mumlarla:** with candles
- **içeriye:** inside (dative)
- **kolunun:** her arm's (possessive)
- **hediye paketi:** gift pack
- **sarılmış:** wrapped (adjective)
- **kutu:** box
- **annem:** my mom
- **tanımış olmalı:** she must have recognized
- **doğum günün kutlu olsun:** happy birthday to you

Questions about the story

1. Öğrenciler Cemile'yi sınıftan dışlarlar çünkü ...

   a) Matematikte oldukça iyidir.
   b) Neşeli bir kızdır.
   c) Kıyafetleri eski ve yırtıktır.
   d) Onu kıskanırlar.

2. Cemile'nin ailesi ne iş yapıyor?

   a) Mevsimlik işçidirler.
   b) İşsizdirler.
   c) Babası madenci, annesi ev hanımıdır.
   d) Öğretmendirler.

3. Cemile, sınıfa girdiğinde herkes onu sıcak karşılar. Doğru mu, yanlış mı?

   a) Doğru.
   b) Yanlış.

4. Cemile sayı saymayı bilmiyor. Doğru mu, yanlış mı?

   a) Doğru.
   b) Yanlış.

5. Anlatıcının annesi sınıfa girdiğinde elinde ... vardır.

   a) Kurabiye ve süt.
   b) Pasta ve mumlar.
   c) Torba dolusu şeker.
   d) Hediye çekleri.

Answers

1) C – Her clothes are worn out and torn.
2) A – They are seasonal workers.
3) B – False.
4) A – True.
5) B – Cake and candles.

Chapter XI

ORMAN — THE FOREST

Ben, bir **ormanım**. İnsanlar böyle **isimlendiriyorlar** beni. **Bilirsiniz**, onlar her şeye bir **isim** verirler; **çınar**, kestane, **akçaağaç**, ladin... **Bence** isimler o kadar da **gerekli** değil. Çünkü ormanda **hepimiz** bir **bütünüz** ve hiçbir zaman **birbirimize** isimlerimizle **seslenmemiz** gerekmiyor.

Ben, bir ormanım. **Kocaman** ve serin. **Bazen** biraz **korkutucu** oluyorum sanırım. **Karanlık** gecelerde buradan **geçen** insanlar **hızlı** hızlı yürüyorlar. **Rüzgar**da sallanan **dallara** bakıyorlar ve birbirlerine "**Acele et**, çabuk **gidelim buradan!**" diyorlar. Bazen **baykuş** onları **sakinleştirmek** için sesleniyor. **O zaman** daha çok **korkuyor** insanlar. İnsanları **anlamak** çok **zor**.

Ben, bir ormanım. Sürekli **değişiyorum. Kışın**, beyaz **elbisemi** giyiyorum ve **çocuklar** için **kar masalları** düşlüyorum. Bu masallarda **tavşanlar**, geyikler ve **tilkiler** var. Çocukların **hayvanları** sevdiğini **biliyorum**. Hayvanlar, benim de **dostum**. Onlara **yiyecek** ve **yuva** veriyorum. **Ağaçlarımın** arasında **koşmaları**, birbirlerine seslenmeleri beni **eğlendiriyor. Bazen kuşlar** biraz **gürültücü** olabiliyor, **sincaplar** da beni **yoruyor**. Kuşlar ve sincaplar böyledir **hep**; her zaman **telaşlı** ve gevezedirler.

Küçük **dereler** geçiyor içimden. **Topraklarımı suluyor** ve ağaçlarımın **büyümesini** sağlıyorlar. **İlkbaharda**, en güzel **çiçeklerim** derelerin **kıyısında** açıyor. **Arılarla** birlikte dereler ve çiçekler için **şarkılar söylüyorum**. O zaman **balıklar,** suyun dışına zıplayıp **selam** veriyorlar bana. Ormanın **şarkısını** bilir misiniz? **Dünyanın** en güzel **korosudur** bu. Bütün **dallar, yapraklar,** çiçekler, hayvanlar **katılır** bu şarkıya.

Bir zamanlar insanların da ormanın şarkısını sevdiklerine **inanıyordum. Artık** insanlardan **korkuyorum** çünkü beni **kandırdılar.** Ben onlara yemyeşil **çimenler verdim** üzerinde oturmaları **için. Sepetlerini** açtılar, örtülerini **yaydılar** ve çimenlerimin üzerinde **yemeklerini yediler.** Teşekkür edeceklerini **düşündüm.** Ama onlar **çöplerini** bırakıp **gittiler.** Beni **temizlemesi** için yağmurdan **yardım istedim.** Yine de **eskisi kadar** temiz olamadım **hiçbir zaman.**

Sonra bir gün **baltalı adamlar** geldi. **Ağaçlarıma** baktılar, **dokundular.** "Bu güzel." dediler. Beni beğendikleri için **sevindim. Uzun** bir **yoldan** gelmişlerdi sanırım. **Yorgundular. Bir şeyler** içtiler ve **uyudular. En serin** gölgemi verdim onlara **dinlenmeleri** için. **Uyanınca** ağaçlarımı **kestiler.** Öyle çok **uğraştım** ki **yeni** ağaçlar **büyütmek** için... Ama yine de **affettim** onları.

Şimdi **çok üzgünüm** ve artık insanları affetmek **istemiyorum.** Kocaman ve **gürültülü** araçlarla gelip bana **saldırdıktan sonra** onlara **küstüm.** Öyle **korkunçtu** ki o gün... Öyle **acımasızdılar** ki! O günden sonra bir **toplantı** yaptık. Hepimiz; ağaçlar, dereler, hayvanlar, **yağmur** ve **bulutlar** bir **karar aldık.** Artık insanları **terk ediyorum. Güzel** ve **yeşil** bir orman **değilim** ben artık. **Belki** bir gün çocuklar beni **hatırlarlar** ve benden af dilerler. Belki **bir gün** insanlar beni **özlerler** ve **değişirler. O zamana kadar** yaşamı **tohumlarımın** içinde **saklayacağım** ve bekleyeceğim.

Hikayenin Özeti

Anlatıcı, bir ormandır. Hayvanların onun içerisinde birlikte nasıl mutlu ve huzurlu bir şekilde yaşadıklarını anlatır. Her tür canlıya barınak ve yiyecek sağlar ancak insanlara kızar çünkü ona çok zarar verirler. Ağaçlarını keserler, çim ve su kaynaklarını kirletirler. İnsanlığa verdiği tüm güzellikler için ormana teşekkür etme zahmetine bile girmezler.

Orman insanların tutumu nedeniyle çok üzülür ve onları affetmek istemez. İnsanlar değişip özür dileyene kadar yaşamı ve güzelliği tohumlarında saklayacağı konusunda kendisine söz verir.

Summary of the story

The narrator is a forest. It describes how happily and peacefully the animals live together in it. It provides shelter and food to all kind of creatures but it is angry with people because they harm it so much. They cut down its trees, pollute its grass and water resources. They don't even bother to thank it for all the beauty that it gives to humanity.

The forest feels very sad because of the attitude of people and doesn't want to forgive them. It promises itself that it will keep the life and beauty hidden in its seeds until people change and apologize.

Vocabulary

- **ormanım:** I am forest
- **isimlendiriyorlar:** they are calling/naming
- **bilirsiniz:** you know (plural/formal)
- **isim:** name
- **çınar:** plane tree
- **akçaağaç:** maple
- **bence:** I think
- **gerekli:** necessary
- **hepimiz:** all of us
- **bütünüz:** we are whole
- **birbirimize:** to each other (dative)
- **seslenmemiz:** that we call
- **ben:** I
- **kocaman:** huge, big
- **bazen:** sometimes
- **korkutucu:** scary
- **karanlık:** dark
- **geçen:** passing by (adjective)
- **hızlı hızlı:** quickly
- **rüzgar:** wind
- **dallara:** branches (dative)
- **acele et:** hurry up (imperative)
- **gidelim buradan:** let's get out of here (optative)
- **baykuş:** owl
- **sakinleştirmek:** to calm, sooth (infinitive)
- **zaman:** then
- **korkuyor:** they get scared
- **anlamak:** to understand (infinitive)
- **zor:** hard
- **değişiyorum:** I am changing
- **kışın:** in winter
- **elbisemi:** my dress (accusative)
- **çocuklar:** children
- **kar:** snow
- **masalları:** tales of (possessive)
- **tavşanlar:** rabbits
- **tilkiler:** foxes
- **hayvanları:** animals (accusative)
- **biliyorum:** I know
- **dostum:** my friend
- **yiyecek:** food
- **yuva:** home

- **ağaçlarımın:** my trees' (possessive)
- **koşmaları:** their running (possessive)
- **eğlendiriyor:** it amuses
- **bazen:** sometimes
- **kuşlar:** birds
- **gürültücü:** noisy
- **sincaplar:** squirrels
- **yoruyor:** it tires [me] out
- **hep:** always
- **telaşlı:** flurried
- **dereler:** streams
- **topraklarımı:** my soils (accusative)
- **suluyor:** it is irrigating
- **büyümesini:** its growth (accusative)
- **ilkbaharda:** in spring (locative)
- **çiçeklerim:** my flowers
- **kıyısında:** along with/on the margin of (locative)
- **arılarla:** with bees
- **şarkılar söylüyorum:** I am singing songs
- **balıklar:** fishes
- **selam veriyorlar:** they are greeting
- **şarkısını:** the song of (accusative)
- **dünyanın:** of the world
- **korosudur:** it is the chorus of
- **dallar:** branches (accusative)
- **yapraklar:** leaves
- **katılır:** it joins
- **bir zamanlar:** once upon a time
- **inanıyordum:** I used to believe
- **artık:** no longer
- **korkuyorum:** I am afraid
- **kandırdılar:** they deceived
- **çimenler:** grasses
- **verdim:** I gave
- **için:** for/to
- **sepetlerini:** their baskets (accusative)
- **yaydılar:** they spread (past tense)
- **yemeklerini yediler:** they ate their meals
- **düşündüm:** I thought
- **çöplerini:** their trash (accusative)
- **gittiler:** they left
- **temizlemesi için:** to clean it
- **yardım istedim:** I asked for help

- **eskisi kadar:** as before
- **hiçbir zaman:** never
- **sonra:** then, after
- **baltalı adamlar:** men with axes
- **ağaçlarıma:** my trees (dative)
- **dokundular:** they touched
- **sevindim:** I got happy
- **uzun:** long
- **yoldan:** from way (ablative)
- **yorgundular:** they were tired
- **bir şeyler:** something
- **uyudular:** they slept
- **en serin:** the coolest
- **dinlenmeleri:** their resting (possessive)
- **uyanınca:** when they woke up
- **kestiler:** they cut
- **uğraştım:** I tried hard
- **yeni:** new
- **büyütmek:** to grow (infinitive)
- **affettim:** I forgave
- **çok üzgünüm:** I'm so sorry
- **istemiyorum:** I don't want
- **gürültülü:** noisy
- **saldırdıktan sonra:** after they attacked
- **küstüm:** I got offended
- **korkunçtu:** it was horrible (past tense)
- **acımasızdılar:** they were ruthless
- **toplantı:** metting
- **yağmur:** rain
- **bulutlar:** clouds
- **karar aldık:** we decided
- **terk ediyorum:** I am leaving
- **güzel:** beautiful
- **yeşil:** green
- **değilim:** I am not
- **belki:** maybe
- **hatırlarlar:** they remember
- **bir gün:** one day
- **özlerler:** they miss
- **değişirler:** they change
- **zamana kadar:** until then
- **tohumlarımın:** my seeds' (possessive)
- **saklayacağım:** I will hide

Questions about the story

1. Hikayede aşağıdaki ağaç isimlerinin hangisinden söz edilmiyor?

   a) Çınar ağacı.
   b) Akçaağaç.
   c) Ladin.
   d) Kızılçam.

2. Orman, insanlardan korkar çünkü ...

   a) İnsanlar, çok gürültü yaparlar.
   b) İnsanlar, ormana zarar verirler.
   c) İçinde yaşayan hayvanları avlarlar.
   d) Sürekli yeni ağaç dikerler.

3. Baykuş, insanları korkutmaya çalışır. Doğru mu, yanlış mı?

   a) Doğru.
   b) Yanlış.

4. Orman, böceklerin gürültücü olduğunu düşünür. Doğru mu, yanlış mı?

   a) Doğru.
   b) Yanlış.

5. Orman, ... bekleyecektir.

   a) Çocukların ormanda oyun oynamasını.
   b) Hayvanların ormana geri dönmesini.
   c) İnsanların ormana evler inşa etmesini.
   d) İnsanların değişmelerini ve onu özlemelerini.

Answers

1) D – Calabrian pine.
2) B – People harm the forest.
3) B – False.
4) B – False.
5) D – People to change and miss it.

Chapter XII

ÇILGIN BİLİM ADAMI — MAD SCIENTIST

Gülten, evin **tek çocuğuydu**. **Çocukluğu**ndan beri **doktor olmak** istiyordu. **Küçükken** sürekli doktor olduğu **oyunlar oynardı**. **Oyuncak bebeklerini** hastası olarak **kullanır**, oyuncak evlerini **hastane** yapardı. Çocukluğunu çeşitli **hastalıkları** ve **yaraları** olan oyuncaklarını **tedavi etmekle** geçirmişti. Günün birinde **gerçek** hastaları olacağını ve onların **hayatlarını kurtaracağını düşlüyordu**.

Gülten, doktor **olabilmek için çalışkan** bir **öğrenci** olması gerektiğinin **farkındaydı**. **Lise** ve üniversite yılları boyunca hep **iyi notlar aldı** çünkü bu notların, iyi bir **tıp fakültesine girmesine yardımcı olacağını** biliyordu. **Ardından** tıp fakültesini **yüksek** bir **ortalamayla** bitirdi. **Çocuk doktoru** oldu. **Evlendi** ve biri kız, biri erkek olmak üzere iki **çocuğu oldu**. Gülten'in **kocası** Murat, mimardı ve aynı zamanda harika bir **aşçıydı**. Gülten'in çocukları da **anneleri gibi** çalışkandılar. Onlara yapmaları **söylenmeden ödevlerini** yaparlar ve **daima** iyi notlar alırlardı. Bir şey **dışında mükemmel** çocuklardı; birbirleriyle sürekli **tartışırlardı**.

O gün Gülten, saat **dört civarı** işten **eve geldi**. **Üstünü değiştirmek** için üst kata çıktı. **Döndüğünde** çocuklar okuldaki günlerinin **nasıl** geçtiği **hakkında** onunla konuşmak için **salonda bekliyorlardı**.
On yaşındaki **oğlu**:
— Bugün, **biyoloji** öğretmenimiz **ölü** bir **kurbağayı** kesmemize **yardım etti**, dedi.

Kurbağaların **akciğer** ve **kalp** gibi ufak **vücut bölümlerini** görmekten **zevk alıyordu.**

— Biyolojiyi seviyorum, **büyüdüğümde biyolog** olmak istiyorum. Ya da **veteriner...** Ya da **mucit...** Bir **ilaç** bulacağım **böylece** hayvanların hepsi **birbirlerini yemeden** yaşamayı **öğrenecek.**

— Çok **saçma! Hayvanlar** birbirlerini yemezlerse **ne yiyecekler?** diye **bağırdı** kız kardeşi.

— Sen **hiçbir şey** bilmiyorsun. Sen bir **kızsın** ve **sadece** dokuz yaşındasın, diyerek **alay etti** oğlan.

— **Kız kardeşine** karşı **nazik ol!** diye **azarladı** onu Gülten.

— **Özür dilerim,** dedi **üzgün** bir yüz ifadesiyle çocuk ve **planını** anlatmaya **devam etti.**

— Bunu **düşündüm tabii ki. Çözüm;** ineklerin ve **koyunların** yaptığı gibi tüm hayvanların **ot yemelerini** sağlayacak bir **hap. Bu şekilde** artık hayvanlar **daha fazla** birbirlerini **yemeyecekler** ve biz de **çimleri biçmek zorunda kalmayacağız.**

— Bu çok **akıllıca!** dedi annesi ve kızına döndü.

— Peki senin **günün nasıl geçti?** diye sordu.

Kız gülümsedi.

— **Her zamanki gibi** anne. Ben, **tanıdığım** bazı kişiler gibi **çılgın** bir **bilim adamı** değil, **senin gibi gerçek** bir doktor **olacağım,** dedi ve ağabeyine **dil çıkardı.**

Hikayenin Özeti

Hikaye, Gülten'in çocukluk anıları ve doktor olma hayali ile başlar. Lisedeki ve üniversitedeki eğitimi sırasında çok çalışmış ve iyi notlar almıştır. Şimdi iki çocuğu olan başarılı bir çocuk doktorudur. Çocukları da anneleri gibi zeki ve çalışkandır.

Bir gün Gülten, işten eve gelir ve çocuklarıyla okulda geçirdikleri gün hakkında konuşmaya başlar. Oğlunun bir planı vardır; büyüdüğünde biyolog veya mucit olmak ister. Böylece tüm hayvanların ot yemelerini sağlayan bir hap icat edebilecektir. Yani artık hayvanlar birbirlerini yemeyecek ve huzur içinde yaşayacaklardır.

Summary of the story

The story begins with childhood memories of Gülten and her dream to be a doctor. She worked hard and got good grades during her education in high school and college. Now she is a successful pediatrician who has two kids. Her kids are smart and hardworking, just like their mother.

One day, Gülten comes home from work and starts to talk to her kids about their day in the school. Her son has a plan: he wants to be a biologist or inventor when he grows up so that he can invent a pill to to make all animals eat grass. So, animals will no longer eat each other and they will live peacefully.

Vocabulary

- **tek çocuğuydu:** she was the only child of (past tense)
- **çocukluğu:** her childhood (possessive)
- **doktor olmak:** to be a doctor
- **küçükken:** when she was young
- **oyunlar oynardı:** she used to play games
- **oyuncak bebeklerini:** her dolls (accusative)
- **kullanır:** she uses
- **hastane:** hospital
- **hastalıkları:** diseases (possessive)
- **yaraları:** injuries (possessive)
- **tedavi etmekle:** with treating
- **gerçek:** real
- **hayatlarını:** their lives (accusative)
- **kurtaracağını:** that she would save (accusative)
- **düşlüyordu:** she was dreaming
- **olabilmek için:** in order to be able to
- **çalışkan:** hardworking
- **öğrenci:** student
- **farkındaydı:** she was aware of
- **lise:** high school
- **iyi notlar:** good grades
- **aldı:** she got
- **tıp fakültesine:** into medical school (dative)
- **girmesine:** for her to get in (dative)
- **yardımcı olacağını:** that it will help (accusative)
- **ardından:** then
- **yüksek:** high
- **ortalamayla:** with grade-point average
- **çocuk doktoru:** pediatrician
- **evlendi:** she got married
- **çocuğu oldu:** she had kid
- **kocası:** her husband
- **aşçıydı:** he was cook (past tense)
- **anneleri gibi:** like their mother

- **söylenmeden:** without being told
- **ödevlerini:** their homeworks (accusative)
- **daima:** always
- **dışında:** but, except
- **mükemmel:** perfect
- **tartışırlardı:** they were used to argue
- **dört civarı:** around four
- **eve geldi:** came home
- **üstünü değiştirmek:** to change her clothes (infinitive)
- **döndüğünde:** when she returned
- **nasıl:** how
- **hakkında:** about
- **salonda:** in the living room (locative)
- **bekliyorlardı:** they were waiting
- **oğlu:** her son
- **biyoloji:** biology
- **ölü:** dead
- **kurbağayı:** frog (accusative)
- **yardım etti:** he helped
- **akciğer:** lung
- **kalp:** heart
- **vücut bölümlerini:** body parts (accusative)
- **zevk alıyordu:** he was enjoying
- **büyüdüğümde:** when I grow up
- **biyolog:** biologist
- **veteriner:** vet
- **mucit:** inventor
- **ilaç:** pill
- **böylece:** so that
- **birbirlerini:** each other (accusative)
- **yemeden:** without eating
- **öğrenecek: they will learn**
- **saçma:** nonsense, absurd
- **hayvanlar:** animals
- **ne yiyecekler:** what are they going to eat
- **bağırdı:** she exclaimed
- **hiçbir şey:** nothing
- **kızsın:** you are girl
- **sadece:** only
- **alay etti:** he taunted
- **kız kardeşine:** to your sister (dative)
- **nazik ol:** be polite (imperative)
- **azarladı:** she admonished
- **özür dilerim:** I'm sorry
- **üzgün:** sad

- **planını:** his plan (accusative)
- **devam etti:** he continued
- **düşündüm:** I thought
- **tabii ki:** of course
- **çözüm:** solution
- **koyunların:** sheep's (plural, possessive)
- **ot:** grass
- **yemelerini:** their eating (accusative)
- **hap:** pill
- **bu şekilde:** thay way (adverb)
- **daha fazla:** no longer, more
- **yemeyecekler:** they will not eat
- **çimleri biçmek:** to mow the lawn (infinitive)
- **zorunda kalmayacağız:** we won't have to
- **akıllıca:** clever
- **günün nasıl geçti:** how was your day
- **her zamanki gibi:** as always
- **tanıdığım:** that I know
- **çılgın:** mad
- **bilim adamı:** scientist
- **senin gibi:** like you
- **gerçek:** real
- **olacağım:** I am going to be
- **dil çıkardı:** she stuck her tongue

Questions about the story

1. Gülten'in uzmanlık alanı nedir?

   a) Nöroloji.
   b) Pediatri.
   c) Kardiyoloji.
   d) Nefroloji.

2. Gülten'in ... çocuğu var.

   a) İki.
   b) Dört.
   c) Üç.
   d) Beş.

3. Gülten'in kocası yemek yapmayı bilmiyor. Doğru mu, yanlış mı?

   a) Doğru.
   b) Yanlış.

4. Erkek çocuk, büyüdüğünde ne olmak istiyor?

   a) Öğretmen.
   b) Doktor.
   c) Pilot.
   d) Bilim Adamı.

5. Çocuk, neden hayvanlar için bir hap bulmak ister?

   a) Hasta hayvanları iyileştirmek için.
   b) Hayvanların birbirlerini yemesini önlemek için.
   c) Ünlü bir bilim adamı olabilmek için.
   d) Hayvanlara yeni yetenekler öğretmek için.

Answers

1) B – Pediatrics.
2) A – Two.
3) B – False.
4) D – Scientist.
5) B – So that he prevents animals from eating each other.

Chapter XIII

DOĞUM GÜNÜ SÜRPRİZİ — THE BİRTHDAY SURPRİSE

Berk'in **doğum günü yaklaşıyordu**. Yıllardır **birlikte** olduğu Selin, onun doğum günü için **güzel** bir şeyler **yapmak istedi**. Berk için **en** güzel **sürprizin ne olabileceğini** düşündü. **Aklına hiçbir şey** gelmeyince ne yapabileceğini Berk'in **yakın arkadaşlarına sordu**. **Ancak** Berk'in arkadaşlarının **önerdiği** hiçbir fikir **hoşuna gitmedi**. **Uzun süredir** birlikte oldukları için Berk'in **kendisini özel** hissetmesini istiyordu. **Sonra** birlikte **vakit geçirmenin** Berk için en güzel doğum günü **hediyesi** olacağına **karar verdi**. Berk'i evine **davet edecekti** ve ona güzel bir **yemek hazırlayacaktı**. Bunun için neler yapabileceğini **düşündü**. **Yemek tarifi** kitaplarını karıştırdı. Sonunda **kararını vermiş** ve geriye yalnızca planını **gerçekleştirmek** kalmıştı.

Berk'in doğum gününde **buluştular** ve beraber **alışveriş** yaptılar. Selin'in Berk **ile** alışverişe gitmesinin **sebebi**, onun o gün en çok **hangi** yemeği **yemek istediğini anlamaktı**. Bu yüzden alışveriş **boyunca** Berk'e sürekli **sorular** sordu:

— **Taze sebze** var, onu alalım. **Hoşuna gitmedi** sanırım, **et**li güzel bir yemek yapayım. Yemeğin **yanında** ne **içsek** daha iyi olur? Senin istediğin **özel bir şey** var mı?

Selin, **dikkatle** Berk'in yüzünü **inceliyor**, onun ne yemek istediğini yüz **ifadesinden anlamaya** çalışıyordu. Berk, **ilgisiz** davrandığında o yiyecekleri **istemediğini**, **gülümsediğinde** ise yemek **istediğini** düşünüyordu. **Sonunda** alışveriş **bitmiş**, Selin ne **pişireceğine** karar vermişti.

Eve **gelir gelmez** Selin, hemen **mutfağa** koştu ve Berk'i **oturma odasına** gönderdi. Berk'e:
—Bir şeye **ihtiyacın olursa** seslen ve **kesinlikle** mutfağa girme, dedi.

Berk, **televizyonun** karşısındaki **koltuğa** doğru yürürken:
— Sen **nasıl istersen.** Çok **acıktım** ve ne yapacağını çok **merak ediyorum**, çabuk ol, dedi.

Selin, gülerek **cevap verdi**:
— **Geçen sefer** yemeği yaktığım için **bu sefer daha dikkatli** olacağım. Bana bu konuda **herhangi** bir şey **söyleme.**

Selin, yemeği **hazırladı.** Mutfakta fazla **tecrübesi** olmadığı için **saatlerce** uğraştı. Berk en sonunda:
— **Eğer** yapamayacaksan dışarıdan **sipariş verebiliriz, kendini yorma**, diye seslendi.

Selin, Berk'in yapmış olduğu **espriye** sinirlenerek:
— **Senin için** uğraşıyorum ve **yemeklerim** çok güzel **olacak.** O nedenle ne kadar **geç olursa olsun** benim yaptığım yemekleri **yiyeceğiz**, dedi.

Selin, biraz **üzülmüştü** ve **gergindi.** Çünkü **yemek hazırlamanın** bu kadar **uzun süreceğini** tahmin etmemişti. Yemekler pişerken **eksik** bazı **malzemeler** olduğunu söyledi ve dışarı çıkıp **frambuazlı** bir **pasta** aldı. Berk'in **durumu** anlamaması için pastayı alışveriş **esnasında** almamıştı. Pastayı **gizlice** evin girişindeki **dolaba koydu.** Bu arada Berk tekrar seslendi:
— Çok acıktım, **hâlâ** hazır olmadı mı? Oturup **sohbet** de edemedik.
— Tamam, yemeğimiz **hazır**, şimdi yiyebiliriz.

Hızlıca yemek masasını hazırladı. Sofraya **mumlar** ve çiçekler koydu. **Bu kadar** çok **bekledikten sonra** her şey hazırdı. Berk, yemeğin çok güzel **olduğuna** ve Selin'in bu kadar **güzel** yemek yaptığına **şaşırdı** ve gülümseyerek:

— Beni mutfağa **almamanın sebebi, başka birini** mutfakta **saklıyor** olman olabilir mi? Başka biri mi **vardı** mutfakta? Senin bu kadar güzel yemek yaptığına **inanamıyorum**, dedi.

Selin, Berk'in bu sözüne sinirlenerek:

— **Beklediğine değdi** sanırım. **Her şeyi kendim** yaptım, dedi.

Yemeğin **sonunda** Selin, **üzerinde mumlar olan** pastayı **getirdi.** Berk, bu duruma çok şaşırdı **çünkü** alışveriş sırasında pasta **almamışlardı.** Selin, pastayı **yerken:**

— **İnanabiliyor musun?** Bir **arkadaşım** frambuazlı pastayı **hiç** sevmediğini söylemişti. İnsan bu kadar güzel bir **şeyi nasıl** sevmez?

Birden Selin'in **aklına** ona frambuazı sevmediğini **söyleyen** bu arkadaşının **kim** olduğu **takıldı. Bir süre** düşündü ve sonunda **kim olduğunu hatırladı.** Bir anda **üzgün** bir ifadeyle Berk'e **baktı:**

— O **sendin.**

Hikayenin Özeti

Berk'in doğum günüdür. Kız arkadaşı ona sürpriz yapmak ister ama aklında hiçbir fikir yoktur. En sonunda birlikte vakit geçirmenin ve Berk'e kendisini özel hissettirmenin en güzel sürpriz olacağına karar verir. Berk'i yemeğe davet eder, birlikte alışverişe çıkarlar. Eve döndüklerinde Selin yemek hazırlamaya başlar. Bu sırada Selin, malzemelerden birinin eksik olduğunu söyler ve dışarı çıkar. Frambuazlı bir pasta alır ve eve geri döner.

Her şey hazırdır. Selin, pastayı ve mumları getirir. Berk, şaşırır çünkü alışverişte pasta almamışlardır. Pastayı yerken Selin'in aklına frambuazı sevmeyen bir arkadaşı olduğu gelir fakat onun kim olduğunu hatırlayamaz. Bir süre düşündükten sonra cevabı bulur.

Summary of the story

It's Berk's birthday. Her girlfriend wants to surprise him but she has no idea. Finally, she decides that it will be the best surprise to spend time together and make Berk feel special. She invites Berk for dinner, they go shopping together. When they get back home, Selin starts cooking. Meanwhile, Selin says that one of the ingredients is missing and she goes out. She buys a rasperry cake and returns home.

Everything is ready, Selin brings the cake and candles. Berk is surprised because they haven't bought a cake during the shopping. While eating the cake, a friend of Selin, who doesn't like raspberries comes to her mind but she can't remember who he/she is. After thinking for a while, she finds the answer.

Vocabulary

- **doğum günü:** birthday
- **yaklaşıyordu:** it was coming up
- **birlikte:** together
- **güzel:** nice, beautiful
- **yapmak:** to do (infinitive)
- **istedi:** she wanted
- **en:** the most
- **sürprizin:** surprise's (possessive)
- **ne olabileceğini:** what it could be (accusative)
- **aklına:** to her mind (dative)
- **hiçbir şey:** nothing
- **yakın arkadaşlarına:** his close friends (dative)
- **sordu:** she asked
- **ancak:** but
- **önerdiği:** that they suggested
- **hoşuna gitmedi:** she didn't like
- **uzun süredir:** for a long time
- **kendisini:** himself (accusative)
- **özel:** special
- **sonra:** then
- **vakit geçirmenin:** of spending time (possessive)
- **hediyesi:** present
- **karar verdi:** she decided
- **davet edecekti:** she would invite
- **yemek hazırlayacaktı:** would prepare meal
- **düşündü:** she thought
- **yemek tarifi:** recipe
- **kararını vermiş:** she has made her decision
- **gerçekleştirmek:** to execute (infinitive)
- **buluştular:** they met
- **alışveriş:** shopping
- **ile:** with
- **sebebi:** reason of (possessive)
- **hangi:** which/what
- **yemek istediğini:** that he wants to eat (accusative)
- **anlamaktı:** it was to understand (past tense)
- **boyunca:** during
- **sorular:** questions
- **taze:** fresh
- **sebze:** vegetable

- **hoşuna gitmedi:** you didn't like
- **et:** meat
- **yanında:** with (locative)
- **içsek:** we should drink
- **özel bir şey:** anything special
- **dikkatle:** carefully
- **inceliyor:** she was examining [his face]
- **ifadesinden:** from his expression (ablative)
- **anlamaya çalışıyordu:** she was trying to understand
- **ilgisiz:** uninterested
- **istemediğini:** that he didn't want (accusative)
- **gülümsediğinde:** when he smiled
- **istediğini:** that he wanted (accusative)
- **sonunda:** finally
- **bitmiş:** it was over (past tense)
- **pişireceğine:** that she will cook (dative)
- **gelir gelmez:** as soon as she comes
- **mutfağa:** to kitchen (dative)
- **oturma odasına:** to living room (dative)
- **ihtiyacın olursa:** if you need
- **kesinlikle:** absolutely
- **televizyonun:** the TV's (possessive)
- **koltuğa:** armchair (dative)
- **nasıl istersen:** however you like
- **acıktım:** I'm hungry
- **merak ediyorum:** I am wondering
- **cevap verdi:** she replied
- **geçen sefer:** last time
- **bu sefer:** this time
- **daha dikkatli:** more careful
- **herhangi:** anything
- **söyleme:** don't tell (imperative)
- **hazırladı:** she prepared
- **tecrübe:** experience
- **saatlerce:** for hours
- **eğer:** if
- **sipariş verebiliriz:** we can order takeout
- **kendini yorma:** don't bother (imperative)
- **espriye:** joke (dative)
- **senin için:** for you
- **yemeklerim:** my foods

- **olacak:** it will be
- **geç:** late
- **olursa olsun:** no matter it is (imperative)
- **yiyeceğiz:** we are going to eat
- **üzülmüştü:** she got upset
- **gergindi:** she was nervous
- **yemek hazırlamanın:** of preparing food (possessive)
- **uzun:** long
- **süreceğini:** that it would would last (accusative)
- **eksik:** missing
- **malzemeler:** ingredients
- **frambuazlı:** (with) raspberry
- **pasta:** cake
- **durumu:** situation (accusative)
- **esnasında:** during
- **almamıştı:** she hadn't bought
- **gizlice:** secretly
- **dolaba:** cupboard (dative)
- **koydu:** she put
- **hâlâ:** still
- **sohbet:** chat
- **hazır:** ready
- **hızlıca:** quickly
- **mumlar:** candles
- **bu kadar:** this much/so much
- **bekledikten:** being waited (ablative)
- **sonra:** after
- **olduğuna:** that it is (dative)
- **güzel:** good
- **şaşırdı:** he was surprised
- **almamanın:** of that you didn't let me (possessive)
- **sebebi:** the reason of (possessive)
- **başka birini:** someone else (accusative)
- **saklıyor:** you were hiding
- **vardı:** was there
- **inanamıyorum:** I can't believe
- **beklediğine:** that you waited (dative)
- **değdi:** it was worth
- **her şeyi:** everything (accusative)
- **kendim:** myself
- **sonunda:** at the end of
- **getirdi:** she brought
- **üzerinde mumlar olan:** with the candles on it
- **getirdi: she brought**
- **çünkü:** because

- **almamışlardı:** they hadn't bought
- **yerken:** while eating
- **inanabiliyor musun:** can you believe
- **arkadaşım:** my friend
- **hiç:** at all
- **sevmediğini:** that he didn't like (accusative)
- **insan:** one, person
- **şeyi:** thing (accusative)
- **nasıl:** how

- **birden:** suddenly
- **aklına:** to her mind (dative)
- **söyleyen:** telling (adjective)
- **takıldı:** it stuck
- **bir süre:** for a while
- **kim olduğunu:** who he was (accusative)
- **hatırladı:** she remembered
- **üzgün:** sad
- **baktı:** she looked at
- **sendin:** it was you

Questions about the story

1. Selin, erkek arkadaşının ne yemek istediğini anlamak için ne yapar?

   a) En yakın arkadaşına sorar.
   b) Arayıp annesine sorar.
   c) Onunla birlikte alışverişe gider.
   d) Sosyal medya profiline bakar.

2. Selin en iyi sürprizin ... olabileceğini düşünür.

   a) Konser bileti almak.
   b) Pahalı bir hediye almak.
   c) Parti vermek.
   d) Birlikte vakit geçirmek.

3. Selin, yemek pişirme konusunda oldukça deneyimlidir. Doğru mu, yanlış mı?

   a) Doğru.
   b) Yanlış.

4. Frambuazlı pasta, Berk'in en sevdiği yiyeceklerden biridir. Doğru mu, yanlış mı?

   a) Doğru.
   b) Yanlış.

5. Selin, ... söylerek evden çıkar.

   a) Doğum günü pastası alacağını.
   b) İşe gittiğini.
   c) Malzemelerden birinin eksik olduğunu.
   d) Komşuyu ziyaret edeceğini.

Answers

1) C – She goes shopping with him.
2) D – Spending time together.
3) B – False.
4) B – False.
5) C – That one of the ingredients is missing.

Chapter XIV

ÖKSÜZ KIZ — THE ORPHAN GİRL

Fatma, **çiftlikte** çalışan **kimsesiz** bir kızdı. **Küçük yaştayken** annesi ve babası **ölmüş**, onu **ninesi** büyütmüştü. Ninesi de **öldüğü zaman** Fatma, bir çiftlikte **hizmetçiliğe** başlamıştı. Çiftliğin **sahipleri** ona para **ödemiyorlar** sadece yemek veriyor ve yatacak **bir yer** sağlıyorlardı.

Fatma, her sabah **erkenden** uyanır ve **işe başlardı**. İnekleri **sağar**, **tarlayı çapalar** ve **kümesi** temizlerdi. Çiftlik **büyüktü** ve **çok fazla iş** vardı. **Akşamüzeri** Fatma çok yorgun olurdu. Fakat çok **çalışkan** bir kız olduğu için çok **yorgun olsa bile** mutlaka evin etrafını **süpürürdü**. Fatma'nın **her günü** böyle geçiyordu ve **akşam** olduğunda yorgunluktan yemeğini **bile** zor bitiriyordu. Erkenden **uyuyordu** ve sabah güneş **doğar doğmaz** kalkıp yine işe başlıyordu.

Fatma bir gün kendisini çok **halsiz** hissetti. **Başı** dönüyordu, ayakta **durmakta** zorlanıyordu. Ama işini **yarım** bırakamazdı. **Elma ağacının** gövdesine **yaslandı**. **Derin** bir **nefes aldı**, birkaç dakika **dinlendi** ve devam etti.

O sırada çiftlik sahibinin **kızı** Leyla oyun **oynuyordu**. Fatma'nın yorgun halini **görünce** ona **yardım etmek** istedi çünkü Fatma'yı seviyordu. Leyla, eline **hemen** bir **süpürge** aldı ve yerleri süpürmeye **başladı**. Fatma bunu görünce **durdu**.

— Leyla **Hanım**, ne yapıyorsunuz? diye sordu.

— Sana **yardım ediyorum**. Ben **bu tarafı** süpürüyorum. Sen de **öbür** tarafı süpür. **Böylece** işin **daha çabuk** bitecek ve sen de **dinleneceksin**, diye cevap verdi Leyla.

— Ama Leyla Hanım, çiftliği süpürmek **sizin işiniz değil**, benim işim, dedi Fatma.

Bunun üzerine **küçük** kız durdu, düşündü.

— Ben de senin gibi **fakir olsaydım** ben de hizmetçilik yapmak **zorunda kalabilirdim**. Herkesin **başına gelebilir** bu. Eğer bir **hizmetçi** olsaydım benim de çok yorgun hissettiğim **günler** olabilirdi. **İşte o zaman ev sahibi**nin kızı bana yardım etse **çok sevinirdim**. İşte **bu yüzden** sana yardım ediyorum.

Fatma, bu **sözleri** duyunca çok **duygulandı**. Çocuğa **sarıldı** ve ona **teşekkür etti**. Leyla ne kadar **iyi** ve **akıllı** bir çocuktu. **İyi ki** Leyla var, diye düşündü. O gece **yatağına** yattığında o kadar **yanlız olmadığını** hissetti çünkü **dünyada** Leyla gibi **iyi insanlar** vardı.

Hikayenin Özeti

Fatma, çiftlikte çalışan yetim bir kızdır. Annesi ve babası o küçükken ölmüş onu ninesi büyütmüştür. Ninesinin ölümü üzerine bu çiftlikte çalışmaya başlamıştır. Arazinin sahipleri Fatma'ya para ödemez sadece yemek ve yatacak bir yer verirler.

Bir gün etrafı süpürürken başı dönmeye başlar. Bunu gören Leyla, ona yardıma koşar. Fatma, durmasını söyler çünkü temizlik onun işi değildir. Küçük kız oldukça iyi kalplidir ve kendisini Fatma'nın yerine koyar.

Summary of the story

Fatma is an orphan girl working in a farm. Her mother and father had died when she was little and her grandma had raised her. Upon the death of her grandma, she started to work in that farm. The owners of the land don't pay her, they just give her food and a place to stay.

One day, while she is sweeping around, she starts to feel dizzy. Seeing that, Leyla rushes to help her. Fatma tells her to stop because it's not her work to do cleaning. The little girl is very nice and she puts herself into Fatma's shoes.

Vocabulary

- **çiftlikte:** in farm (locative)
- **kimsesiz:** orphan
- **küçük yaştayken:** when she was at a young age
- **ölmüş:** she/she had passed away
- **ninesi:** her grandma
- **öldüğü zaman:** when she died
- **hizmetçiliğe:** working as a maid (dative)
- **sahipleri:** owners (possessive)
- **ödemiyorlar:** they aren't paying
- **bir yer:** a place
- **erkenden:** early
- **işe başlardı:** she was used to start working
- **sağar:** she milks
- **tarlayı:** field (accusative)
- **çapalar:** she hoes
- **kümesi:** coop (accusative)
- **büyüktü:** it was big (past tense)
- **çok fazla:** a lot of
- **akşamüzeri:** towards the evening
- **çalışkan:** hardworking
- **yorgun:** tired
- **olsa bile:** even though she is
- **süpürürdü:** she was used to sweep
- **her günü:** her every day
- **akşam:** at night
- **bile:** even
- **uyuyordu:** she was used to sleep
- **doğar doğmaz:** as soon as [the sun] rises
- **halsiz:** weak
- **başı:** her head
- **durmakta:** standing (locative)
- **yarım:** incomplete, unfinished
- **elma ağacı:** apple tree
- **yaslandı:** she leaned
- **derin:** deep
- **nefes aldı:** she took a breath
- **dinlendi:** she rested
- **sırada:** meanwhile
- **kızı:** the daughter of

- **oynuyordu:** she was playing
- **görünce:** when she saw
- **yardım etmek:** to help (infinitive)
- **hemen:** immediately
- **süpürge:** broom
- **başladı:** she started
- **durdu:** she stopped
- **hanım:** Ms.
- **yardım ediyorum:** I am helping
- **bu tarafı:** that side (accusative)
- **öbür:** other
- **böylece:** so
- **daha çabuk:** faster
- **dinleneceksin:** you will take a rest
- **sizin işiniz değil:** it's not your job
- **küçük:** little
- **fakir:** poor
- **olsaydım:** If I were
- **zorunda kalabilirdim:** I might have to
- **başına gelebilir:** one can happen to
- **hizmetçi:** maid
- **günler:** days
- **işte o zaman:** then only then
- **ev sahibi:** landlord
- **çok sevinirdim:** I would be happy
- **bu yüzden:** so
- **sözleri:** her words
- **duygulandı:** she got emotional
- **sarıldı:** she hugged
- **teşekkür etti:** she thanked
- **iyi:** nice
- **akıllı:** smart
- **iyi ki:** so glad
- **yatağına:** to her bed (dative)
- **yanlız olmadığını:** that she was not alone (accusative)
- **dünyada:** in the world (locative)
- **iyi insanlar:** good people

Questions about the story

1. **Başı dönmeye başladığında Fatma ne yapıyordu?**

    a) Müzik dinliyordu.

    b) Leyla ile sohbet ediyordu.

    c) Yemek yiyordu.

    d) Etrafı süpürüyordu.

2. **Fatma, nerede yaşamaktadır?**

    a) Villada.

    b) Malikânede.

    c) Çiftlikte.

    d) Apartmanda.

3. **Çiftliğin sahipleri Fatma'ya çok para öderler. Doğru mu, yanlış mı?**

    a) Doğru.

    b) Yanlış.

4. **Fatma, kendisine küçük kızın yardım etme teklifine karşı çıktı çünkü ...**

    a) Yaptığı iş çok kolaydı.

    b) Bu Fatma'nın işiydi.

    c) Kızın onunla alay edeceğini düşündü.

    d) Evin hanımının ona kızacağını düşündü.

5. **Fatma, çiftlikte yalnız olmadığını ne zaman fark etti?**

    a) Leyla ona yardım ettiğinde.

    b) Diğer hizmetçilerle birlikte vakit geçirdiğinde

    c) Dua ettiğinde.

    d) Küçük kızla oyun oynadığında.

Answers

1) D – She was sweeping around.
2) C – In a farm.
3) B – False.
4) B – It was Fatma's job.
5) A – When Leyla helped her.

Chapter XV
İŞ GÖRÜŞMESİ — THE JOB INTERVİEW

Ozan, **neredeyse** iki senedir **düzenli** bir işte çalışmamıştı. Bugün Ozan için **büyük gündü** çünkü bir **iş görüşmesine** gidiyordu. Bu sefer **umutluydu**, işi **alacağını** düşünüyordu. **Telefonda** konuştuğu **sekreter**in sesi oldukça **samimi** ve **cesaret verici** gelmişti.

Ozan, **çevirmendi**. Parmakları **klavyenin** üzerinde adeta **dans** ederdi. Fakat insanlarla olan **ilişkileri, yazma yeteneği** kadar iyi **değildi**. Sivri **dili** bazen başına **bela açardı**. **Son** işinde **patronu** ona **her sabah** kendisi için **kahve yapmasını** söylemişti. Ozan **gülmüştü** buna.

— Kahve **yapmayacağım**, bu benim **işimin** bir **parçası** değil, demişti.

— **Sözleşmeyi** yeniden **oku**, senin işin **ben ne dersem** o, diye yanıtlamıştı patronu.

— Bu kadın işi, **kendin yap**, demişti Ozan.

Ozan **binadan** ayrılırken patronu **hâlâ** arkasından **bağırıyordu**. Patronunu **azarlamak** çok **hoşuna gitmişti**. Fakat birkaç gün **sonra** işsizlik **gerçeğiyle yüzleşmek** zorunda kaldı. **Kirasını** ve **elektrik faturalarını** ödemek ve yemek yapmak için bir şeyler **almak zorundaydı**. Ne yapacaktı?

Patronundan **özür dilemeyi** ve işini **geri istemeyi** düşündü. **Ama** bu durum ona çok **utanç verici** görünüyordu. **Parası bitmişken** bunun **nasıl** görüneceğini **kim umursardı** ki? **Birkaç** hafta daha **düşündükten** sonra **sonunda** patronunu **aradı** ve **özür diledi**. Patronu özrünü **kabul etti** ama **başka birini işe aldığını** söyledi.

Bunun üzerine Ozan, **geçici** bir iş bulmak için bir **iş bulma kurumuyla temasa geçti**. Fakat **gönderildiği** hiçbir **şirket** yeni bir **eleman** aramıyordu. **Bu yüzden nihayet düzenli bir iş** için görüşmeye gideceğinden dolayı **heyecanlıydı**.

Ozan'ın iş görüşmesine giderken yaşadıkları oldukça **moral bozucuydu**. **Yolculuğu** sırasında **trafik sıkışıktı** ve görüşmenin olacağı **mahalle tekinsiz** bir yerdi. Ozan'ın oraya **varması** 45 dakika **sürmüştü** ve bina **duvar yazılarıyla** doluydu.

Neyse ki Ozan, **maceralı** yolculuğuna **rağmen** görüşmeye **zamanında** gitti. Ama onu **beklettiler** ve **müdürle** yapacağı görüşme **yarım saat geç** başladı. Özür dileme **zahmetine bile girmeyen** müdür, bir **sigara yaktı** ve kahvesinden bir **yudum aldı**. Sandalyesine **yaslandı** ve ayaklarını **masaya koydu**. Ozan'a **bir sürü** soru **sordu**. Ozan, **her** sorunun **bir öncekinden** daha **aptalca** olduğunu düşünüyordu. **Son soru** ise şuydu: "**Bundan** on yıl sonra **nerede** olmak **istiyorsun**?"

"Bu sorunun tercümanlıkla **ne ilgisi var**?'' diye düşündü Ozan. **Berbat** bir mahallede, **kaba** bir **adamdan** aptalca **sorular**! **On yıl** sonra nerede olmak isterdi ki?

— Bu **çöplük** dışında **herhangi bir yerde**! dedi öfkeyle.

Ayağa **kalktı** ve oradan **uzaklaştı**.

Hikayenin Özeti

Ozan, uzun zamandır düzenli bir işte çalışmamıştır. Büyük gün gelmiştir çünkü Ozan bir iş görüşmesine gidecektir. Ozan çevirmendir ve yazma becerileri oldukça iyidir. Son işinde patronu, kendisine her sabah kahve hazırlamasını ister ama Ozan bunu reddeder. Bu yüzden tartışırlar ve Ozan işi bırakır. Birkaç hafta sonra Ozan'ın parası biter ve patronunu arayıp işini geri istemeye karar verir. Fakat patronu, onun yerine başka birini işe aldıklarını söyler.

Ozan'ın yeni iş görüşmesi, 30 dakika geç başlar ve müdür oldukça kaba bir adamdır. Ozan'ın aptalca olduğunu düşündüğü birçok soru sorar. Son sorudan sonra Ozan sinirlenir ve binayı terk eder.

Summary of the story

Ozan has not worked in a steady for a long time. Today is a big day because he is going to a job interview. He is a translator and his typing skills are very good. At his last job, his boss had told him to make a coffee for him every morning but Ozan had refused. So they had an argument and he quit the job. After couple weeks, he runs out of of money and decides to call his boss and ask for his job back. However, his boss says that he had already hired a replacement.

The interview for the new job starts 30 minutes late and the manager is a very rude man. He asks Ozan a lot questions, which Ozan finds stupid. After the final question, Ozan gets mad and leaves the building.

Vocabulary

- **neredeyse:** almost
- **düzenli:** steady
- **büyük gündü:** it was the big day (past tense)
- **iş görüşmesine:** to job interview (dative)
- **umutluydu:** he was hopeful
- **alacağını:** that he will get (accusative)
- **telefonda:** on the phone (locative)
- **sekreter:** secretary
- **samimi:** friendly
- **cesaret verici:** encouraging
- **çevirmendi:** he was a translator (past tense)
- **klavyenin:** the keyboard's (possessive)
- **dans ederdi:** he was used to dance
- **ilişkileri:** his relations
- **yazma yeteneği:** his typing skill
- **değildi:** it was not
- **dili:** his tongue
- **bela açardı:** it caused trouble

- **son:** last
- **patronu:** his boss
- **her sabah:** every morning
- **kahve yapmasını:** him to make coffee (accusative)
- **gülmüştü:** he had laughed
- **yapmayacağım:** I am not going to make
- **işimin:** my job's (possessive)
- **parçası:** part of
- **sözleşmeyi:** contract (accusative)
- **oku:** read (imperative)
- **ben ne dersem:** anything I say
- **kendin yap:** do it yourself (imperative)
- **binadan:** out of the building (ablative)
- **hâlâ:** still
- **bağırıyordu:** he was yelling
- **azarlamak:** to tell off, to reprimand (infinitive)
- **hoşuna gitmişti:** it felt good
- **sonra:** later

- **gerçeğiyle:** with the reality of
- **yüzleşmek:** to face (infinitive)
- **kirasını:** rent (accusative)
- **elektrik faturalarını:** utility bills (accusative)
- **almak:** to buy (infinitive)
- **zorundaydı:** he had to
- **özür dilemeyi:** apologizing (accusative)
- **geri istemeyi:** asking back (accusative)
- **ama:** but
- **utanç verici:** embarrassing
- **parası bitmişken:** when he run out of money
- **nasıl:** how
- **kim umursardı:** who would care
- **birkaç:** couple
- **düşündükten:** he has been thinking (ablative)
- **sonunda:** finally
- **aradı:** he called
- **özür diledi:** he apologized
- **kabul etti:** he accepted
- **başka birini:** somebody else (accusative)
- **işe aldığını:** that he hired (accusative)

- **geçici:** temporary
- **iş bulma kurumuyla:** with the job-creating agency
- **temasa geçti:** he contacted
- **gönderildiği:** that he was sent
- **şirket:** company
- **eleman:** employee
- **bu yüzden:** so
- **nihayet:** finally
- **düzenli bir iş:** a steady job
- **heyecanlıydı:** he was excited
- **moral bozucuydu:** it was disappointing
- **yolculuğu:** his travel
- **trafik sıkışıktı:** traffic was congested
- **mahalle:** neigborhood
- **tekinsizdi:** it was rough (past tense)
- **varması:** him to get (possessive)
- **sürmüştü:** it took
- **duvar yazılarıyla:** graffiti (plural)
- **neyse ki:** fortunately
- **maceralı:** adventurous
- **rağmen:** despite
- **zamanında:** in time

- **beklettiler:** they made [him] wait
- **müdürle:** with the manager
- **yarım saat:** half an hour
- **geç:** late
- **zahmetine bile girmeyen:** without bothering
- **sigara yaktı:** he lit a cigarette
- **yudum aldı:** he took a sip
- **yaslandı:** he leaned back
- **masaya:** on the desk (dative)
- **koydu:** he put
- **bir sürü:** a lot of
- **sordu:** he asked
- **her:** each
- **bir öncekinden:** than the preceding one (ablative)
- **aptalca:** stupid (adjective)
- **son soru:** the final question
- **bundan:** from now
- **nerede:** where (locative)
- **istiyorsun:** you want
- **ne ilgisi var:** what does [that] have to do with
- **berbat:** lousy
- **kaba:** rude
- **adamdan:** from man (ablative)
- **sorular:** questions
- **on yıl:** ten years
- **çöplük:** dump
- **herhangi bir yerde:** anywhere (locative)
- **kalktı:** he stood up
- **uzaklaştı:** he walked out

Questions about the story

1. **Ozan, ... düzenli bir işte çalışmamıştır.**

    a) İki senedir.

    b) İki gündür.

    c) İki aydır.

    d) İki haftadır.

2. **Patronu ondan her sabah ... yapmasını istemiştir.**

    a) Sandviç.

    b) Çay.

    c) Kahve.

    d) Çorba.

3. **Ozan, neden patronundan özür diledi?**

    a) Çünkü işe geç kaldı.

    b) Çünkü işini geri almak istedi.

    c) Çünkü soğuk kahve getirdi.

    d) Çünkü iş arkadaşıyla tartıştı.

4. **Görüşmenin yapılacağı binaya varmak ne kadar sürdü?**

    a) 25 dakika.

    b) 15 dakika.

    c) 55 dakika.

    d) 45 dakika.

5. **Müdürün hangi sorusu Ozan'ı sinirlendirdi?**

    a) Bu işi almak için uygun özelliklere sahip misin?

    b) Terfi almak istiyor musun?

    c) Bundan 10 sene sonra nerede olmak istiyorsun?

    d) Son işinde ne kadar çalıştın?

Answers

1) A – For two years.
2) C – Coffee.
3) B – Because he wanted to get his job back.
4) D – 45 minutes.
5) C – Where do you want to be 10 years from now on?

Chapter XVI

OKULU ASMAK —
SKİPPİNG THE SCHOOL

Günlerdir hava **açık** ve **güneşliydi**. Bu durum **lise** üçüncü sınıfa giden **gençleri** çok mutlu etmişti ama **böyle güzel** bir **havada derse girmek hoşlarına gitmiyordu**. Güzel bir salı **sabahında** Adnan'ın **aklına** bir **fikir** geldi.

Teneffüste sürekli birlikte **vakit geçirdiği** arkadaşları Can, Mehmet, Burcu Gözde ve Özlem'e:

— **Bugün** çok güzel ve **sıcak** bir gün. Okulda **olmayı** hiç **istemiyorum**, artık çok **sıkıldım**. Öğleden sonra **yalnızca** iki **dersimiz** var, bugün **okulu asabiliriz**, dedi.

Mehmet, **çalışkan** ve **düzenli** bir çocuktu. Bu nedenle **bu fikre** hemen **karşı çıktı**.

— Okulu asmak sizce de **kötü** bir şey **değil mi**? Üstelik bunu **öğrendiklerinde** ailemiz bize **ne der**? Biliyorsunuz ki **önümüzdeki sene** üniversite **sınavlarına** gireceğiz. O nedenle **derslerimizi** sıkı bir şekilde **takip etmeliyiz**.

Grubun yaramaz çocuğu Can hemen **cevap verdi**.

— **Seneye** üniversite **sınavına gireceğimiz için** zaten hiçbir yere **gidemeyeceğiz**. Bunun **farkındasındır** umarım. Bu güzel **zamanları iyi değerlendirme**miz lazım. **Ne olur** bir gün okulu assak? Güzel bir gün geçiririz. **Okuldan eve** döndüğümüz saatte de ayrılırız. **Kimsenin** olan bitenden **haberi olmaz**. Hem sen de iyi bir **öğrenci olmaya** biraz **ara** vermiş olursun.

Can'ın bu **sözlerine** herkes **güldü**. **Aslında** bu fikir herkesin **kafasına yatmıştı. Öğleden sonraki** dersleri **asacaklar** ve tüm öğleden sonra **dışarıda** vakit geçireceklerdi. **Öğle yemeğini** okulda yediler ve bu arada **nereye gideceklerini** konuştular. **Sonunda** şehrin yakınında ve **yürüme mesafesindeki ormanlık alana** gitmeye **karar verdiler.** Önce **yol** üzerindeki **markete** uğradılar, **içecek** ve **atıştırmalık** bir şeyler aldılar. Marketten çıktıklarında Burcu'nun **dikkatini** bir **fayton** çekti. Faytondan **müzik** sesleri geliyordu ve üzerinde hiç **yolcu** yoktu. Burcu **heyecanla:**

— **Bakın** bir fayton! Ben **daha önce** hiç **binmedim.** Gideceğimiz **yere** faytonla mı **gitsek**? dedi.

Özlem hemen **karşı çıktı.**

— Fayton mu? Sen **aklını mı kaçırdın**? Ben **atlar**dan çok **korkarım.** Üstelik **görmüyor musun** ne kadar **küçük** bu fayton. Bu kadar insan onun içine **nasıl sığarız**?

Gözde hemen **en yakın arkadaşı** Burcu'yu **savunmaya** geçti.

— Burcu daha önce hiç faytona **binmediğini söylüyor.** Ne olur binsek? Hem **sırtımızdaki** çantalarla ve marketten **aldığımız** onca **şeyle** yürümek çok **yorucu** olabilir. Şimdi Adnan, **faytoncu** ile anlaşır. Onun **ne kadar iyi pazarlık** ettiğini bilirsiniz. Böylece çok **ucuza** gidebiliriz.

Adnan hemen **atıldı** ve faytoncu ile pazarlığa **başladı.** Faytoncuya **öğrenci olduklarını** ve fazla **paralarının** olmadığını söyledi. Onları ormanlık alana **götürmesi** için **adamı ikna etti.** Gençler müzik **eşliğinde** ormanlık alana **vardılar.** Burası **şehirde** yaşayanların **boş zamanlarında** geldikleri ve **eğlendikleri** geniş bir alandı. **Piknik yapmak** için masalar, **mangal** yerleri ve **yürüyüş yolları** vardı. Baharın gelmesiyle **her yer yemyeşil** olmuştu. **Güneş**, ağaçların **yaprakları** arasından **çimlerin üzerine vuruyordu. Kelebekler** uçuşuyor, kuşlar **cıvıldıyordu.** Bu manzarayı **görünce** çok mutlu oldular ve sabahki **teklifi** için Adnan'a **teşekkür ettiler.**

Ormanlık alanın yanından bir **nehir** akıyordu. Nehrin kenarındaki **kumsala** doğru giden gençler, orada **oturup** marketten **aldıkları** yiyecekleri ve içecekleri **tükettiler**. Burada **espriler** yaparak, okul **anılarından** ve biraz da **hoşlandıkları kişilerden** bahsederek **vakit geçirdiler**. **Sohbete** dalarak zamanın **nasıl geçtiğini** anlamayan gençler, Mehmet'in uyarısı ile hemen toplandılar.

— Okulun **bitiş saati** geldi, **hemen** eve **dönmeliyiz**. **Ailemiz** okulu astığımızı **anlamamalı**.

Hızlıca etrafı **toplayıp çantalarını** yanlarına **aldılar**. Güzel bir gün **geçirmenin** verdiği **mutlulukla evlerine** doğru **yola çıktılar**.

Hikayenin Özeti

Güneşli bir günde altı arkadaş okulu asmaya karar verir. Aralarından birisi bu fikre karşı çıkar çünkü yakında sınava gireceklerdir ve ona odaklanmaları gerekir. Sonunda hepsi ikna olur. Öğle yemeğini okulda yerler ve nereye gidecekleri konusunda plan yaparlar. Ormanlık alana gitmeye karar verirler ve okuldan ayrılırlar.

Yolda giderken bir fayton görürler ve ormanlık alana onunla giderler. Vardıklarında kendilerine oturup sohbet edecekleri güzel bir yer ararlar. Güzel vakit geçirdikten sonra öğrencilerden biri eve dönme vaktinin geldiği söyler. Eşyalarını toplayıp evlerine doğru yola çıkarlar.

Summary of the story

On a sunny day, six friends decide to skip the school. One of them opposes this idea because they will take an exam soon and they should focus on it. At last, they are all convinced. They have lunch at school and make plan on where to go. They decide to go to woods and leave the school.

On the way, they see a carriage and they go to the woods by the carriage. When they arrive, they look for a nice place to sit and chat. After having good time, one of the students says that it is time to return home. They pick their belongings and head to their homes.

Vocabulary

- **günlerdir:** for days
- **açık:** clear
- **güneşliydi:** it was sunny (past tense)
- **lise:** high school
- **gençleri:** youngsters (accusative)
- **böyle:** such
- **güzel:** beautiful
- **havada:** in the weather (locative)
- **derse girmek:** to attend a class
- **hoşlarına gitmiyordu:** they didn't like
- **sabah:** morning
- **aklına:** to his mind (dative)
- **fikir:** idea
- **teneffüste:** in the break (locative)
- **vakit geçirdiği:** that he spends time
- **bugün:** today
- **sıcak:** hot
- **olmayı:** to be (accusative)
- **hiç istemiyorum:** I don't want at all
- **sıkıldım:** I'm bored
- **yalnızca:** only
- **dersimiz:** our class
- **okulu asabiliriz:** we can skip the school
- **çalışkan:** hardworking
- **düzenli:** neat
- **bu fikre:** that idea (dative)
- **karşı çıktı:** he opposed
- **kötü:** bad
- **değil mi:** isn't it
- **üstelik:** also
- **öğrendiklerinde:** when they find out
- **ne der:** what would they say
- **biliyorsunuz:** you know
- **önümüzdeki sene:** the coming year
- **sınavlarına:** exams of (dative)
- **derslerimizi:** our classes (accusative)
- **takip etmeliyiz:** we should follow
- **grubun:** of the group
- **yaramaz:** mischievous
- **cevap verdi:** he replied
- **seneye:** the next year

- **sınavına gireceğimiz için:** as we will take the exam
- **gidemeyeceğiz:** we won't be able to go
- **farkındasındır:** you might be aware
- **zamanları:** times (accusative)
- **iyi değerlendirme:** making the best of (noun)
- **ne olur:** what happens if
- **okuldan:** from the school (ablative)
- **eve:** to home (dative)
- **kimsenin:** nobody's (possessive)
- **haberi olmaz:** he/she doesn't find out
- **öğrenci:** student
- **olmaya:** to be (dative)
- **ara:** break
- **sözlerine:** his words (dative)
- **güldü:** he/she laughed
- **aslında:** actually, in fact
- **kafasına yatmıştı:** [the idea] sounded plausible to him/her
- **öğleden sonraki:** in the afternoon
- **asacaklar:** they would skip
- **dışarıda:** outside (locative)
- **öğle yemeğini:** lunch (possessive)
- **nereye:** where (dative)
- **gideceklerini:** that they will go (accusative)
- **sonunda:** finally
- **yürüme mesafesindeki:** within walking distance
- **ormanlık alan:** woods
- **karar verdiler:** they decided
- **yol:** way
- **markete:** to market (dative)
- **içecek:** beverage
- **atıştırmalık:** snack
- **dikkatini:** her attention (accusative)
- **fayton:** carriage
- **müzik:** music
- **yolcu:** passenger
- **heyecanla:** with excitement
- **bakın:** look
- **daha önce:** before
- **binmedim:** I haven't taken
- **yere:** to the place (dative)
- **gitsek:** we should go
- **karşı çıktı:** she objected

- **aklını mı kaçırdın:** did you lose your mind
- **atlar:** horses
- **korkarım:** I'm afraid of
- **görmüyor musun:** don't you see
- **küçük:** small
- **nasıl:** how
- **sığarız:** we fit
- **en yakın arkadaşı:** her best friend
- **savunmaya:** to defend (dative)
- **binmediğini:** that she haven't been in (accusative)
- **söylüyor:** she tells
- **sırtımızdaki:** on our backs
- **aldığımız:** that we bought
- **şeyle:** with stuff
- **yorucu:** tiring
- **faytoncu:** coachman
- **ne kadar iyi:** how well
- **pazarlık:** bargain
- **ucuza:** cheaply
- **atıldı:** he came forward
- **başladı:** he started
- **öğrenci olduklarını:** that they are student (accusative)
- **paraları:** their money
- **götürmesi:** him to take [them] (possessive)
- **adamı:** the man (accusative)
- **ikna etti:** he convinced
- **eşliğinde:** accompanied by
- **vardılar:** they arrived
- **şehirde:** in the city (locative)
- **boş zamanlarında:** in their spare time (locative)
- **eğlendikleri:** that they have fun
- **piknik yapmak:** to have a picnic (infinitive)
- **mangal:** barbeque
- **yürüyüş yolları:** walking trails
- **her yer:** everywhere
- **yemyeşil:** very green
- **güneş:** sun
- **yaprakları:** leaves of (possessive)
- **çimlerin üzerine:** on the grass (dative)
- **vuruyordu:** it was beating down on
- **kelebekler:** butterflies
- **cıvıldıyordu:** it was chirping
- **görünce:** when he/she saw
- **teklifi:** offer

- **teşekkür ettiler:** they thanked
- **nehir:** river
- **kumsala:** to beach (dative)
- **oturup:** sat (adverb)
- **aldıkları:** that they bought
- **tükettiler:** they consumed
- **espriler:** jokes
- **anılarından:** their memories
- **hoşlandıkları kişilerden:** people they liked
- **vakit geçirdiler:** they spent time
- **sohbete:** chat (dative)
- **nasıl geçtiğini:** that how it passed (accusative)
- **bitiş saati:** ending time
- **hemen:** right now
- **dönmeliyiz:** we should go back
- **ailemiz:** our family
- **anlamamalı:** he/she shouldn't realize
- **toplayıp:** packed (adverb)
- **çantalarını:** their bags (accusative)
- **aldılar:** they took
- **geçirmenin:** of spending
- **mutluluk:** happiness
- **evlerine:** to their homes (dative)
- **yola çıktılar:** they headed

Questions about the story

1. Pikniğe kaç öğrenci gider?

   a) Beş.
   b) Dört.
   c) Altı.
   d) Üç.

2. Mehmet, okulu asma fikrine neden karşı çıkar?

   a) gün hastadır.
   b) Dersleri kaçırmak istemez.
   c) Yapması gereken ödevleri vardır.
   d) Babası okul müdürüdür.

3. Gittikleri yerde büyük bir göl vardır. Doğru mu, yanlış mı?

   a) Doğru.
   b) Yanlış.

4. Özlem, faytona binmek istemez çünkü ...

   a) Atlardan korkar.
   b) Hayvanlara eziyet edilmesini istemez.
   c) Faytoncuya verecek parası yoktur.
   d) Yürüyerek gitmek ister.

5. Öğrenciler, ... okulu astıklarını öğrenmesini istemezler.

   a) Öğretmenlerinin.
   b) Ailelerinin.
   c) Okul müdürünün.
   d) Diğer arkadaşlarının.

Answers

1) C – Six.
2) B – He doesn't want to miss classes.
3) B – False.
4) A – She is afraid of horses.
5) B – Their families.

Chapter XVII

BABA VE OĞUL — FATHER AND SON

Sinan, onlarla **kalan** babası **yüzünden, evlendiğinden beri** eşiyle **sürekli** tartışıyordu. **Eşi** onun babasını istemiyordu. Yine **böyle** bir **tartışma** sırasında eşi:

— **Ya** ben giderim **ya da** baban gider. **Birlikte** yaşamamız **mümkün değil**, demişti.

Sinan, eşini **kaybetmeyi göze alamazdı**. Babası yüzünden **çıkan** tartışmalar **dışında** eşiyle **aralarında** bir **problem yoktu**. Onunla evlenebilmek için çok **mücadele etmişti**, ailesini bu evliliğe **ikna etmek** için **aylarca uğraşmıştı**. Eşini ve **çocuklarını** çok seviyordu. Onlar **olmadan** yaşayamazdı.

Çaresizlik içinde **ne yapacağını** düşündü ve sonunda bir **çözüm** yolu **buldu**. Babasını, **yıllar önce** yaptırdığı **dağ evine götürecekti**. Haftada **birkaç kez uğrayacaktı** ve ne ihtiyacı olursa **karşılayacaktı**. Böylelikle eşiyle arasındaki **sorunlar bitecekti**.

Babasının **ihtiyaç duyabileceği** tüm **malzemeleri** hazırladı. Onu **yatağından** kaldırdı ve **arabaya** kadar yürümesine **yardım etti. Yaşlı** adam **zor** yürüyordu. **Tüm** bunları **izleyen oğlu** Can:

— Baba, ben de **sizinle** gelmek **istiyorum**, dedi.

— Hava **çok soğuk**. Ben, dedeni **yeni evine bırakıp** hemen **döneceğim**, diye cevap verdi Mehmet.

Küçük çocuk **ısrar etti**. Can, **inatçı** bir **çocuktu. Şimdi** de **onlarla birlikte** gelmek için **ağlamaya başlamıştı**. Sinan **biraz** düşündü.

Can'ın onlarla gelmesi **belki** de **daha iyi** olurdu. Can, **yol boyunca** konuşur, dedesinin **üzüntüsünü hafifletirdi** belki. **Sonunda** çocuğun gelmesine **razı oldu**.

Kar yağıyordu. Tipi yüzünden **yolu görmek** gittikçe **zorlaşmıştı.** Bu yüzden **ağır ağır** gidiyorlardı. Can, **durmadan** bir şeyler **anlatıyordu.** Sinan, oğlunu **dinlerken dikiz aynasından** babasına **baktı.** Yaşlı adam **suskundu. Nereye** götürüldüğünü **anlamıştı. Ağlıyordu** ama kimseye **belli etmemeye çalışıyordu.**

Saatler süren **yolculuktan** sonra dağ evine **ulaştılar.** Sinan, **uzun süredir** buraya **gelmemişti.** Evi **temizledi,** yatağı **hazırladı.** Evden **getirdiği** yiyecekleri mutfağa **koyduktan sonra** babasını **yatağa** yerleştirdi. Hava o kadar soğuktu ki **sobayı** yakmasına **rağmen** oda **ısınmamıştı.** Babası **üşüyordu.** Dışarıdan biraz daha **odun** getirdi, sobanın **yanına** koydu. Babası burada **tek başına nasıl yaşayacaktı?** Çaresizlik içinde babasına baktı.

Artık **gitme zamanıydı. Hava kararıyordu** ve **karın şiddeti** artmıştı. Babasına doğru **eğildi,** onun **yanaklarını** ve ellerini **öptü.** "Beni **affet!**" der gibi **sarıldı.** Ağlamaya başladı. Babası **da** ağlıyordu. "Buna **mecburum.**" demek **istedi** ama diyemedi. Oğlunun **elinden tuttu** ve odayı **terk etti.** Yola çıktıklarında Can ağlamaya başlamıştı.

— Dedemi **neden** orada **bıraktık?** diye sordu çocuk.

Sinan'ın verecek hiçbir **cevabı yoktu.** "Annen **böyle** istiyor." **diyemiyordu.**

— Sen **yaşlandığında** ben de seni **buraya** mı **getireceğim**? diye sordu oğlu.

Bu soruyu **duyunca** kendisini **çok kötü hissetti.** Sinan, **direksiyonu** ani bir hareketle **çevirdi** ve arabayı dağ evine doğru **sürdü.** Eve **ulaştıklarında** babasının **boynuna** sarıldı.

— **Affet beni** baba! Beni affet! **Sana** bunu **yaptığım için** beni affet! diyerek ağladı.

— **Geri geleceğini** biliyordum **oğlum.** Ben babamı yanlızlığa **terk etmedim** ki bunu sen **niye yapasın.** Beni burada **bırakmayacağını** biliyordum, dedi babası.

Hikayenin Özeti

Sinan, eşiyle sürekli tartışır çünkü Sinan'ın babası onlarla birlikte kalıyordur. Sinan, bu problemi nasıl çözeceğini bir süre düşünür. Sonunda babasını dağ evine götürmeye ve onu orada bırakmaya karar verir. Babasına hiçbir şey söylemez. Gerekli hazırlıkları yapar, babasının ihtiyaç duyacağı her şeyi alır. Bu sırada oğlu da onlarla gelmek ister.

Dağ evi yolunda Sinan'ın babası nereye gittiklerini anlar ve ağlamaya başlar. Vardıklarında Sinan babası için uygun ortamı hazırlar, getirdiği eşyaları eve yerleştirir. Evden oğluyla birlikte ayrılır. Oğlunun sorusu üzerine Sinan kendisini çok kötü hisseder ve yaptığından pişman olur. Geri dönüp babasından özür diler.

Summary of the story

Sinan constantly argues with his wife because Sinan's father stays with them. He thinks about how to solve this problem for a while. Finally, he decides to take his father to the chalet and leave him there. He doesn't say anything to his father. He makes the necessary preparations, takes everything that his father will need.

On the way to the chalet, Sinan's father understands where they are going and starts to cry. When they arrive, Sinan prepares the ideal environment for his father, puts the stuff he brought. He leaves the house with his son. Upon the question of his son, Sinan feels very bad and regrets what he has done. He goes back and apologizes to his father.

Vocabulary

- **kalan:** staying (adjective)
- **evlendiğinden beri:** since he got married
- **yüzünden:** because of
- **sürekli:** always
- **eşi:** his wife
- **böyle:** such
- **tartışma:** argument
- **ya:** either
- **ya da:** or
- **birlikte:** together
- **mümkün değil:** it's not possible
- **kaybetmeyi:** losing (accusative)
- **göze alamazdı:** he couldn't run the risk
- **çıkan:** that arised (adjective)
- **dışında:** except
- **aralarında:** between them (locative)
- **problem yoktu:** there was no problem
- **mücadele etmişti:** he had fought
- **ikna etmek:** to convince (infinitive)

- **aylarca:** for months
- **uğraşmıştı:** he had strived
- **çocuklarını:** his kids (accusative)
- **olmadan:** without
- **çaresizlik:** despair
- **ne yapacağını:** what he will do (accusative)
- **çözüm:** solution
- **buldu:** he found
- **yıllar önce:** years ago
- **dağ evine:** chalet, cottage (dative)
- **götürecekti:** he would take
- **birkaç kez:** couple times
- **uğrayacaktı:** he would visit
- **karşılayacaktı:** he would meet [his needs]
- **sorunlar:** problems
- **bitecekti:** it would be over
- **ihtiyaç duyabileceği:** that he might need
- **malzemeleri:** materials (accusative)
- **yatağından:** from his bed (ablative)
- **arabaya:** to the car (dative)
- **yardım etti:** he helped

- **yaşlı**: old
- **zor**: barely
- **tüm**: all
- **izleyen**: watching (adjective)
- **oğlu**: his son
- **sizinle**: with you (plural/formal)
- **istiyorum**: I want
- **çok soğuk**: it is very cold
- **yeni evine**: to his new house (dative)
- **bırakıp**: dropping [him] off (adverb)
- **döneceğim**: I will be back
- **küçük**: little
- **ısrar etti**: he insisted
- **inatçı**: stubborn
- **çocuktu**: he was kid (past tense)
- **şimdi**: now
- **onlarla birlikte**: with them
- **ağlamaya**: crying (dative)
- **başlamıştı**: he had started
- **biraz**: a little, some
- **belki**: maybe
- **daha iyi**: better
- **yol boyunca**: along the way
- **üzüntüsünü**: his sorrow (accusative)
- **hafifletirdi**: it would ease
- **sonunda**: finally
- **razı oldu**: he consented
- **kar yağıyordu**: it was snowing
- **tipi**: blizzard
- **yolu**: the road (accusative)
- **görmek**: to see (infinitive)
- **zorlaşmıştı**: it had become harder
- **ağır ağır**: slowly
- **durmadan**: steadily
- **anlatıyordu**: he was telling
- **dinlerken**: while listening
- **dikiz aynasından**: in rearview mirror (ablative)
- **baktı**: he looked
- **suskundu**: he was silent (past tense)
- **nereye**: where (dative)
- **anlamıştı**: he understood
- **ağlıyordu**: he was crying
- **belli etmemeye**: not to show (dative)
- **çalışıyordu**: he was trying
- **saatler**: hours
- **yolculuktan**: travel (ablative)
- **ulaştılar**: they arrived
- **uzun süredir**: for a long time

- **gelmemişti:** he hadn't been
- **temizledi:** he cleaned
- **hazırladı:** he prepared
- **getirdiği:** that he brought
- **koyduktan sonra:** after he put
- **yatağa:** to the bed (dative)
- **sobayı:** stove (accusative)
- **rağmen:** even though
- **ısınmamıştı:** it didn't get warm
- **üşüyordu:** he was cold
- **odun:** wood
- **yanına:** next to (dative)
- **tek başına:** on his own
- **nasıl yaşayacaktı:** how would he live
- **gitme zamanıydı:** it was time to go
- **hava kararıyordu:** it was getting dark
- **karın şiddeti:** snow intensity
- **eğildi:** he leaned
- **yanaklarını:** his cheeks (accusative)
- **öptü:** he kissed
- **affet:** forgive (imperative)
- **sarıldı:** he hugged
- **da:** too
- **mecburum:** I have to
- **istedi:** he wanted
- **elinden tuttu:** holded his [son's] hand
- **terk etti:** he left
- **neden:** why
- **bıraktık:** we left
- **cevabı:** his answer (possessive)
- **yoktu:** there was no
- **böyle:** so
- **diyemiyordu:** he couldn't say
- **yaşlandığında:** when you get old
- **buraya:** here (dative)
- **getireceğim:** I will bring
- **duyunca:** when he heard
- **çok kötü:** so bad
- **hissetti:** he felt
- **direksiyonu:** the wheel (accusative)
- **çevirdi:** he turned
- **sürdü:** he drove
- **ulaştıklarında:** when they arrived
- **boynuna:** to his neck (dative)
- **affet beni:** forgive me (imperative)
- **sana:** to you (dative)

- **yaptığım için:** for what I did
- **geri geleceğini:** that you will come back (accusative)
- **oğlum:** my son
- **terk etmedim:** I didn't leave
- **niye yapasın:** why would you do (optative)
- **bırakmayacağını:** you wouldn't leave me (accusative)

Questions about the story

1. **Sinan, eşiyle neden tartışır?**

   a) Eşi, hiç yemek yapmaz.
   b) Sinan, onunla yeterince ilgilenmez.
   c) Eşi, ondan pahalı hediyeler almasını ister.
   d) Eşi, onun babasını evde istemez.

2. **Sinan, babasını ... götürür.**

   a) Dağ evine.
   b) Yazlığa.
   c) Köyüne.
   d) Yeni evine.

3. **Sinan'ın eşi de onlarla birlikte gider. Doğru mu, yanlış mı?**

   a) Doğru.
   b) Yanlış.

4. **Sinan, arabayı dağ evine sürerken hava nasıldı?**

   a) Yağmur yağıyordu.
   b) Kar yağıyordu.
   c) Güneşliydi.
   d) Sisliydi.

5. **Sinan'ın eşi de onlarla birlikte gider. Doğru mu, yanlış mı?**

   a) Doğru.
   b) Yanlış.

6. **Sinan'ın, dağ evine geri dönmesinin sebebi neydi?**

   a) Hava çok kötüydü.
   b) Babasını özledi.
   c) Evde bir şey unuttu.
   d) Can'ın sözleri onu üzdü.

Answers

1) D – His wife doesn't want his father at home.
2) A – To the chalet.
3) B – False.
4) B – It was snowing.
5) D – False.
6) D – Can's words made him sad.

Chapter XVIII

KÜÇÜK KEDİ — THE LİTTLE CAT

Ferhat ile **sevgilisi** Sultan, **hafta sonu** dışarı çıkmak için **plan yapmışlardı.** Ferhat, Sultan'la buluşacağı için çok **heyecanlıydı.** Yeni **ütülediği** gömleğini ve siyah **pantolonunu** giydi. Özenle **saçlarını taradı, parfümünü** sıktı. Sultan'ın **yaşadığı** eve doğru **yola çıktı.** Fakat Sultan'ın kapısını **çaldığında** kapıyı **açan olmadı.** Bunun üzerine Ferhat, **pencereye** doğru **seslendi:**

— **Aşkım** ben geldim, **hazır mısın?** Sultan cevap versene! Bugün **beraber** vakit geçireceğimizi **unuttun mu?**

Sultan elinde **saç maşasıyla aşağı** baktı.

— Neden **bağırıyorsun? Hazırlanıyorum,** o nedenle kapıyı açamadım. Sana güzel **görünmeye** çalışıyorum. Çok **sabırsızsın.**

Ferhat da biraz **utangaç** bir ifadeyle:

— Ben, **buluşacağımızı** unuttun **sandım.** Bu yüzden telaşlandım. **Tamam o zaman** sen hazırlan, ben seni **kapıda bekliyorum.**

Ferhat, **bir süre** daha Sultan'ı bekledi ama **gelen giden yoktu.** Bu sırada **sokağı** izlemeye başladı. Uzaktan bir **kedinin** sesi **geliyordu. Etrafına** bakındı. Sokağın köşesinde **beyaz yavru** bir kedi **gördü.** Kedi, bir şey istiyormuş **gibi** sürekli **miyavlıyordu.** Ferhat, **hemen** kedinin yanına **koştu.** Ne kadar da **zayıftı.** Kedinin haline **üzüldü.**

— Canım benim, **ne yapıyorsun** sen burada? Niye böyle **ağlıyormuş gibi** miyavlıyorsun? Sen çok **tatlı** küçük bir kedisin. **Karnın mı aç** yoksa senin?

Ferhat, kediyi **sevmek** istedi. O **yaklaştıkça** kedi, kendisine bir **zarar** geleceğini sanarak **kaçıyordu**. Ferhat, kediye yaklaşmaya **devam etti**. Sevmek için **elini uzattı**. Kedi **köşeye** sıkışmıştı ve daha fazla **gidecek yeri kalmamıştı**. En sonunda Ferhat'ın elini **tırmaladı**. Ferhat **acıyla haykırdı**.

— Ah! Elim çok **acıyor**. **Kanıyor** sanırım.

Ferhat'ın **çığlıkları** tüm sokakta **yankılanıyordu**. Sultan, **sokaktan gelen** bağırışları **duyunca** pencereden **dışarı** baktı. **Elini tutarak** haykıran Ferhat'ı gördü.

— Ferhat, **bu halin ne?** Ne oldu sana, **neden** bağırıyorsun? Bu **yüzünün hali ne?**

Ferhat **acı içinde kıvranarak** cevap verdi.

— Çok soru **soruyorsun! Baksana** halime. Elim kanıyor. **Şu kedi,** elimi tırmaladı.

Sultan, Ferhat'ın sözlerine kızdı.

— **Hay Allah!** Kediyle **ne işin var** senin? Neden **sakin** sakin kapının önünde beni **beklemedin?** Bir de bana **sesini yükseltiyorsun.**

Ferhat'ın acısı biraz **hafiflemişti**. Sultana seslendi:

— Tamam, sinirlenmene **gerek yok**. Şimdi **lütfen aşağı in** ve elim için bir şeyler **getir**.

Sultan, aceleyle **ecza dolabının** yanına gitti. **Pansuman** için gerekli olan **oksijenli suyu, pamuğu** ve **yara bandını aldı. Hemen aşağı indi. Ferhat bu sırada küçük kediye bakıyordu. Zavallıcık, bir çöp kutusunun arka**sına **saklanmıştı**. Kediyle **konuşmaya** başladı.

— Görüyor musun **yaptığını?** Sen miyavlayıp **durduğun** için ben de sana **acıdım**, seni biraz sevmek istedim. **Senin yüzünden** sevgilimle **geçireceğim** günüm **mahvoldu**. Elimdeki şu **yaraya** bak.

Sultan, bir yandan **pansuman yapıyordu** bir yandan da Ferhat'a **gülüyordu**. Fakat en sonunda **sabrı taştı**.

— **Yeter** artık, **küçücük** kediyi neden **suçluyorsun?** Zavallıcık senin **söylediklerini anlayamaz**, üstelik **suç sende**. Neden küçücük hayvanı **rahatsız ediyordun?** Şimdi sızlanmaya **hakkın yok**.

Sultan **konuşurken** sokağın başında **büyük** bir kedi **belirdi**. Yavru kedinin yanına gelerek onun **tüylerini yalamaya** başladı. **O da** küçük kedi **gibi** beyazdı. Bunu gören Sultan:

— **Bak**, kedi **muhtemelen** annesini **bulamadığı** için miyavlıyordu. **Görüyor musun, annesi** yanına gelince sustu. **Şu haline bak**. Benden sana bir **tavsiye**; bir daha asla **hayvanları** rahatsız etme. Onları kendi hallerine **bırak**. Hayatlarına **saygı duy**.

Ferhat, Sultan'a baktı ve **kolunu** onun **beline doladı**.

— Sen de beni **bir daha** bu kadar çok **bekletme**, dedi.

Hikayenin Özeti

Ferhat ve Sultan, hafta sonu dışarı çıkmaya karar verirler. Ferhat, Sultan'ın evine gider ve kapının önünde onu beklemeye başlar. Beklerken küçük bir kedi görür ve onu sevmeye çalışır. Kedi korkar ve Ferhat'ın elini tırmalar. Ferhat, acı içinde bağırırken Sultan, onu duyar ve ne olduğunu sorar. Ferhat, neler olduğunu anlatır ve Sultan'dan yardım ister.

Sultan, aşağı inip Ferhat'ın eline pansuman yapar. Bu sırada anne kedi görünür ve gelip yavrusunu yalamaya başlar. Bunu gören Sultan, Ferhat'a hayvanları rahatsız etmemesi konusunda tavsiye verir. Ferhat da Sultan'dan onu bir daha bekletmemesini ister.

Summary of the story

Ferhat and Sultan decide to go out for the weekend. Ferhat goes to Sultan's house and starts to wait for her in front of the door. While he is waiting, he sees a little cat and tries to pet it. The cat gets scared and scratches Ferhat's hand. Sultan hears him while he is crying out in pain and she asks what is going on. He tells her what happened and asks for her help.

Sultan goes down and dresses Ferhat's hand. Meanwhile, the mother cat appears and starts to lick its baby. Seeing that, Sultan advises Ferhat not to disturb animals. Then, Ferhat asks her not to make him wait again.

Vocabulary

- **sevgilisi:** his girlfriend
- **hafta sonu:** on the weekend
- **plan yapmışlardı:** they had planned
- **heyecanlıydı:** he was excited
- **ütülediği:** that he ironed
- **pantolonunu:** his pants (accusative)
- **saçlarını taradı:** he combed his hair
- **parfümünü:** his perfume (accusative)
- **yaşadığı:** that she lives
- **yola çıktı:** he headed
- **çaldığında:** when he knocked
- **açan olmadı:** no one opened
- **pencereye:** to window (dative)
- **seslendi:** he called out
- **aşkım:** my love (interjection)
- **hazır mısın:** are you ready
- **beraber:** together
- **unuttun mu:** did you forget

- **saç maşası:** curling iron
- **aşağı:** down
- **bağırıyorsun:** you are shouting
- **hazırlanıyorum:** I'm getting ready
- **görünmeye:** to look (dative)
- **sabırsızsın:** you are impatient
- **utangaç:** shy
- **buluşacağımızı:** that we will meet (accusative)
- **sandım:** I thought
- **tamam o zaman:** okay then
- **kapıda:** at the door (locative)
- **bekliyorum:** I am waiting
- **bir süre:** for a while
- **gelen giden yoktu:** there was nobody passing by
- **sokağı:** the street (accusative)
- **kedinin:** the cat's (possessive)
- **geliyordu:** it was coming
- **etrafına:** around (dative)
- **beyaz:** white

- **yavru:** baby [animal]
- **gördü:** he saw
- **gibi:** as if
- **miyavlıyordu:** it was meowing
- **hemen:** straight away
- **koştu:** he ran
- **zayıftı:** it was weak (past tense)
- **üzüldü:** he felt sorry
- **ne yapıyorsun:** what are you doing
- **ağlıyormuş gibi:** as if crying
- **tatlı:** cute
- **karnın mı aç:** are you hungry
- **sevmek:** to pet (infinitive)
- **yaklaştıkça:** as he got closer
- **zarar:** harm
- **kaçıyordu:** it was running away
- **devam etti:** he kept
- **elini:** his hand (accusative)
- **uzattı:** he put out his hand
- **köşeye:** in the corner (dative)
- **gidecek yeri kalmamıştı:** there was nowhere left for it to go
- **tırmaladı:** it scratched
- **acıyla:** rackingly
- **haykırdı:** he cried out
- **acıyor:** it hurts
- **kanıyor:** it is bleeding
- **çığlıkları:** his screams
- **yankılanıyordu:** it was echoing
- **sokaktan:** from the street (ablative)
- **gelen:** coming (adjective)
- **duyunca:** when she heard
- **dışarı:** out
- **elini tutarak:** holding his hand (adverb)
- **bu halin ne:** what happened to you
- **neden:** why
- **yüzünün hali ne:** what's with your face
- **acı içinde:** in pain
- **kıvranarak:** writhing (adverb)
- **soruyorsun:** you are asking
- **baksana:** look (imperative)
- **şu kedi:** that cat
- **hay Allah:** oh God!
- **ne işin var:** what are you doing
- **sakin:** calmly
- **beklemedin:** you didn't wait

- **sesini:** your voice (accusative)
- **yükseltiyorsun:** you are raising
- **hafiflemişti:** it was relieved
- **gerek yok:** there is no need
- **lütfen:** please (interjection)
- **aşağı in:** come down (imperative)
- **getir:** bring (imperative)
- **ecza dolabı:** first aid cabinet
- **pansuman:** medical dressing
- **oksijenli suyu:** peroxide (accusative)
- **pamuğu:** cotton (accusative)
- **yara bandını:** bandage (accusative)
- **bu sırada:** meanwhile
- **zavallıcık:** poor
- **çöp kutusu:** rubbish bin
- **saklanmıştı:** it was hid
- **konuşmaya:** to talk (dative)
- **yaptığını:** what you have done (accusative)
- **durduğun:** that you kept
- **acıdım:** I felt pity
- **senin yüzünden:** because of you
- **geçireceğim:** that I would spend
- **mahvoldu:** it got ruined
- **yaraya:** to the wound (dative)
- **pansuman yapıyordu:** she was dressing
- **gülüyordu:** she was laughing
- **sabrı taştı:** she had enough
- **yeter:** enough (interjection)
- **küçücük:** so tiny
- **suçluyorsun:** you are blaming
- **söylediklerini:** what you are saying (accusative)
- **anlayamaz:** it can't understand
- **suç sende:** it's your fault
- **rahatsız ediyordun:** you were disturbing
- **hakkın yok:** you have no right
- **konuşurken:** while she was talking
- **büyük:** big
- **belirdi:** it appeared
- **tüylerini:** its fluffs (accusative)
- **yalamaya:** licking (dative)

- **da:** it was also
- **gibi:** like
- **bak:** see
- **muhtemelen:** probably
- **bulamadığı:** that it couldn't find
- **görüyor musun:** do you see
- **annesi:** its mom
- **şu haline bak:** look at you (imperative)
- **tavsiye:** advice
- **hayvanları:** animals (accusative)
- **bırak:** leave (imperative)
- **saygı duy:** respect (imperative)
- **kolunu:** his arm (accusative)
- **beline:** her waist (dative)
- **doladı:** he wrapped
- **bir daha:** again
- **bekletme:** don't make [me] wait (imperative)

Questions about the story

1. Ferhat, Sultan'ı beklerken o ne yapıyordu?
   a) Kediyi seviyordu.
   b) Yemek yapıyordu.
   c) Çamaşır yıkıyordu.
   d) Hazırlanıyordu.

2. Ferhat, kedinin miyavladığını görünce ... düşündü.
   a) Kedinin kaybolduğunu.
   b) Kedinin aç olduğunu.
   c) Kedinin yaralı olduğunu.
   d) Annesini aradığını.

3. Sultan, Ferhat'ın yarasına pansuman yaptı. Doğru mu, yanlış mı?
   a) Doğru.
   b) Yanlış.

4. Kedi, nasıl tepki gösterir?
   a) Ferhat'ın elini tırmalar.
   b) Sultan'ı ısırır.
   c) Kaçar.
   d) Ferhat'ın onu sevmesine izin verir.

5. Sultan, Ferhat'ın yarasına pansuman yaptı. Doğru mu, yanlış mı?
   a) Doğru.
   b) Yanlış.

6. Sultan, Ferhat'a ... tavsiye eder.
   a) Sakin olmasını.
   b) Hayvanları sevmesini.
   c) Hayvanların yaşamına saygı göstermesini.
   d) Kendisine hediye almasını.

Answers

1) D – She was getting ready.
2) B – That the cat was hungry.
3) A – True.
4) A – It scratches Ferhat's hand.
5) C – True.
6) C – To respect the life of animals.

Chapter XIX

OTEL — THE HOTEL

Orta yaşlı bir çift, lüks bir otelde **yer ayırtmıştı**. Otelde **sekiz** gece **kalacaklardı**. Gelir gelmez odalarına **çıkmak** istediler. Otel **müşterilerine** sunulan "hoş geldiniz" **içkisini** ve diğer **ikramları** geri çevirdiler. Yorgunlardı, **dinlenmek** istiyorlardı. **Nazik** insanlara benziyorlardı. Oteli **övmüşler**, bahçeyi çok **beğendiklerini** söylemişlerdi.

Otel **müdürü** Seyhan, **her şeyin** onlar odalarına çıktıktan **yaklaşık** on dakika sonra **başladığını** anlatıyor:

— **Birden** bağırışlar duyduk. **Asansör**ün kapısı gürültüyle **açıldı**. Karı koca, ikisinin de **yüzleri** öfkeden **kızarmıştı**. Kucaklarında **çarşaflar** vardı. İnanabiliyor musunuz? Odadaki çarşafları, **yastık kılıflarını** ve yatak örtülerini **lobiye** getirmişlerdi.

Seyhan, **daha önce** hiç böyle bir şeyle **karşılaşmamıştı**. Bazen müşterilerin **şikayet ettikleri** şeyler oluyordu **elbette**. Bazıları **yemekleri** beğenmezdi, bazıları kendilerine verilen odanın **manzarasını**... Ama **sorunlar** için bir **çare** bulunurdu **her zaman**. Seyhan, işinde **tecrübeliydi**. Müşterileri nasıl **memnun edeceğini** iyi bilirdi. Bu kez de sorunu **çözmek** için çiftin yanına gitti hemen.

—Problem neydi? diye sordu.

— Yataklarımız **leş gibi**! Bu nasıl bir **rezillik**?

Seyhan inanamıyordu. Yastık kılıflarını, **çarşafları** aşağıya kadar **getirmeye** ne gerek vardı? Oteldeki diğer **misafirler** olayı izliyor, **aralarında** konuşuyorlardı. **Karı koca** o kadar **sinirliydiler** ki

Seyhan'ın söylediklerini **dinlemiyorlardı** bile. En **sonunda** Seyhan'ın sabrı taştı. Çifte **odalarının** sabah **temizlendiğini** ve yatak takımlarının **değişmiş** olduğunu söyledi.

— Ben **yatak takımlarında** bir problem **göremiyorum**, dedi Seyhan. Belki de size öyle geldi.

— **Burada** kalmak için **bir sürü** para ödüyoruz. Bizden **şüphe** mi ediyorsun? **Kanıt mı göstermemiz gerekiyor** sana? Biz yatakların **pis** olduğunu **söylüyorsak** pistir. **İhtiyacın olan** tek kanıt bu, diye **bağırdı** kadın.

Seyhan, daha fazla konuşmadı ve **oda servisini** aradı. Yatak örtüleri **hemen** değiştirildi. Bu arada olaya **tanık olan** yeni bir müşteri oda tutmaktan **vazgeçmiş**, bir **başka** müşteri ise **ayrılmak** istediğini söylemişti.

— **Steril** bir **ortam** istiyorlardı, diye anlattı Seyhan. **Hastanede** ya da belki **ameliyathanede** oda ayırtmaları **daha iyi olurdu**. Bu otel **temiz** ama bir ameliyathane kadar değil.

Olaylar bununla bitmemişti. **Bir sonraki** akşam, çiftin yeni bir **talebi** vardı. Bu kez yedi **kutu** sprey **dezenfektan** istediler.

— **Her gece** için birer kutu dezenfektana **ihtiyacımız var.** Telefonu, televizyonu, tüm **kapı kollarını**, musluğu ve odamıza giren **otel personelini** dezenfekte etmemiz gerekiyor.

Seyhan çok **şaşırmıştı**. Otel personelini **dezenfekte etmek…** Bu, ne **saçma** bir istekti? Çiftin sekiz gece için **rezervasyon** yapmış olduğunu **hatırladı**. Hayır, bu saçmalıklara daha fazla **dayanmasına** imkan yoktu. **Derin** bir **nefes** aldı, gülümsedi. Çifte diğer caddede onlar için **daha uygun**, çok temiz bir otel olduğunu **kibarca** söyledi. Karı koca birbirlerine **bakıyorlardı**. Seyhan, onların **cevap** vermelerini bile **beklemedi**. Diğer oteli **aradı** ve "çok temiz" bir oda **ayırttı**. Çifte **ulaşım** için **endişelenmemelerini** söyledi. Otelin **limuzini** onları **yeni** otellerine götürecekti.

— **Farklı** bir otel **önerdiğim** için şaşırmış **görünüyorlardı.** Ama otelde kaldıkları **ikinci gün** için onlardan **ücret istemeyişimizden** ve limuzin **hizmetinden** hoşlandılar, dedi Seyhan.

Hikayenin Özeti

Orta yaşlı bir çift, bir otelde sekiz gün kalmak için oda ayırtmıştır. Çift otele gelir ve odalarına çıkar. Fakat bir problem vardır; daha ilk günden odalarındaki bütün çarşafları, yastık kılıflarını lobiye getirip bırakırlar. Otelin müdürü Seyhan, ne olduğunu sorduğunda yatak örtülerinin pis olduğunu ve değiştirilmesini istediklerini söylerler. Seyhan, oda servisini arar ve örtüler hemen değiştirilir.

Fakat bir sonraki akşam çift yeniden lobiye gelir. Odalarındaki tüm mobilyalara ve hatta odalarına giren otel çalışanlarına sıkmak için bir sürü dezenfektan sprey isterler. Ertesi günlerde çiftin isteyebileceği şeyler endişelenen Seyhan, onlara başka bir otelde kalmalarını söyler.

Summary of the story

A middle-aged couple has booked a room for eight-day stay in a hotel. They come to the hotel and go up to their rooms. However, there is a problem: on the very first day, they bring all the sheets and pillowcases to lobby and drop them there. When Seyhan asks what the problem is, they say that their bedding is dirty and they want it replaced. Seyhan calls room service and the bedding is replaced.

However, the couple comes to lobby the next evening again and demands a lot of spray disinfectant to spray on furnitures in the room and even hotel staff entering their room. Worried about what the couple might want in the following days, Seyhan tells them to stay in another hotel.

Vocabulary

- **orta yaşlı:** middle-aged
- **yer ayırtmıştı:** he/she had booked
- **sekiz:** eight
- **kalacaklardı:** they would stay
- **çıkmak:** to go up (infinitive)
- **müşterilerine:** customers (dative)
- **içkisini:** drink of (accusative)
- **ikramları:** refreshments (accusative)
- **dinlenmek:** to rest (infinitive)
- **nazik:** kind
- **övmüşler:** they praised
- **beğendiklerini:** that they liked (accusative)
- **müdürü:** manager of
- **her şeyin:** of everything
- **yaklaşık:** almost
- **başladığını:** that it started (accusative)
- **birden:** suddenly
- **asansör:** elevator
- **açıldı:** it opened
- **yüzleri:** their faces

- **kızarmıştı:** they had turned red
- **çarşaflar:** sheets
- **yastık kılıflarını:** pillowcases (accusative)
- **lobiye:** to lobby (dative)
- **daha önce:** before
- **karşılaşmamıştı:** she hadn't encountered
- **şikayet ettikleri:** that they complain
- **elbette:** of course
- **yemekleri:** food (accusative)
- **manzara:** landscape
- **sorunlar:** problems
- **çare:** solution
- **her zaman:** everytime
- **tecrübeliydi:** she was experienced
- **memnun edeceğini:** that she will satisfy (accusative)
- **çözmek:** to solve (infinitive)
- **leş gibi:** filthy, stinking
- **rezillik:** disgrace
- **çarşafları:** the sheets (accusative)
- **getirmeye:** to bring (dative)

- **misafirler:** guests
- **aralarında:** to each other/in between them (locative)
- **karı koca:** man and wife
- **sinirliydiler:** they were angry
- **dinlemiyorlardı:** they were not listening
- **sonunda:** at last
- **odalarının:** their room's (possessive)
- **temizlendiğini:** that it was cleaned (accusative)
- **değişmiş:** it was replaced
- **yatak takımlarında:** beddings (locative)
- **göremiyorum:** I can't see
- **burada:** here (locative)
- **bir sürü:** a lot of
- **şüphe:** doubt
- **kanıt:** proof
- **göstermemiz gerekiyor:** we must show
- **pis:** dirty
- **söylüyorsak:** if we say
- **ihtiyacın olan:** that you need
- **bağırdı:** she shouted
- **oda servisini:** room service (accusative)

- **hemen:** immediately
- **tanık olan:** that witnessed
- **vazgeçmiş:** he/she gave up
- **başka:** other, else
- **ayrılmak:** to leave (infinitive)
- **steril:** sterile
- **ortam:** environment
- **hastanede:** in hospital (locative)
- **ameliyathanede:** in operating room (locative)
- **daha iyi olurdu:** it would be better
- **temiz:** clean
- **bir sonraki:** the next
- **talebi:** his/her request (possessive)
- **kutu:** can
- **dezenfektan:** disinfectant
- **her gece:** each night
- **ihtiyacımız var:** we need
- **kapı kollarını:** door handles (accusative)
- **otel personelini:** hotel staff (accusative)
- **şaşırmıştı:** she was shocked
- **dezenfekte etmek:** to disinfect (infinitive)
- **saçma:** nonsense
- **rezervasyon:** booking

- **hatırladı:** she remembered
- **dayanmasına:** her to stand (dative)
- **derin:** deep
- **nefes:** breath
- **daha uygun:** more suitable
- **kibarca:** politely
- **bakıyorlardı:** they were looking at
- **cevap:** answer
- **beklemedi:** she didn't wait
- **aradı:** she called
- **çok temiz:** very clean
- **ayırttı:** she booked
- **ulaşım:** transportation
- **endişelenmemelerini:** them to not worry (accusative)
- **limuzin:** limousine
- **yeni:** new
- **farklı:** different
- **önerdiğim:** that I suggested
- **görünüyorlardı:** they seemed
- **ikinci gün:** second day
- **ücret istemeyişimizden:** that we didn't charge (ablative)
- **hizmetinden:** service (ablative)

Questions about the story

1. Çift, otelde kaç gün kalmak için yer ayırtmıştı?

   a) Beş.
   b) Sekiz.
   c) Altı.
   d) Dokuz.

2. Seyhan, otelde ... olarak çalışır.

   a) Oda servisi.
   b) Müdür.
   c) Barmeyd.
   d) Resepsiyonist.

3. Çift, ilk gün odadaki ... kirli olduğunu iddia eder.

   a) Masanın.
   b) Pencerelerin.
   c) Klozetin.
   d) Yatak örtülerinin.

4. Seyhan, bir sonraki gece için de çiftten para aldı. Doğru mu, yanlış mı?

   a) Doğru.
   b) Yanlış.

5. Seyhan, çifte ... önerdi.

   a) Odalarını değiştirmelerini.
   b) Oteli değiştirmelerini.
   c) Fikirlerini değiştirmelerini.
   d) Kıyafetlerini değiştirmelerini.

Answers

1) D – Nine.
2) B – Manager.
3) D – The beddings.
4) B – False.
5) B – To change the hotel.

Chapter XX

YÜZÜK — THE RİNG

Aşağı yukarı ayda bir kez, **işim** dolayısıyla İzmir'e gitmem gerekiyordu. Bir gün İzmir'e **vardığımda** bir şeyler yemek için bir **lokantaya** girdim. **Genellikle aynı** lokantaya giderdim ve beni **tanıyorlardı.** Garson, **ceketimi** alıp başka bir odaya **götürdü.** Lokantaya gelen tüm **müşterilerin** ceketlerini bu odadaki **askıya** asıyorlardı.

Yemeğimi **yedim**, lokantada **beni** tanıyan çalışanlarla **muhabbet ettim.** Bir saat kadar sonra çıkmaya **hazırdım.** Yemeklerin parasını **ödedim** ve garsondan ceketimi **getirmesini** istedim.

Garson, geri döndüğünde:
— Ceketi **giyecek** misiniz yoksa elinizde mi **taşıyacaksınız** efendim? diye sordu.
— **Bugün** hava oldukça güzel, **elimde** taşıyacağım, diye **yanıtladım.**

Ceketi garsondan **aldığım sırada** yere bir şey **düştü.** Garson, düşen şeyi **eğilip aldı** ve bana **verdi.**
— **Buyrun** efendim, dedi ve bana **küçük** beyaz bir **kutu** verdi.
Elimdeki kutuya **bakarak:**
— **Bu ne?** Bu kutu **benim değil.** Onu daha önce hiç **görmedim,** dedim.
— Ama **sizin** ceketinizden düştü. **Düştüğünü** siz de gördünüz, değil mi?

Haklıydı fakat **yanlış** bir şey vardı. Elimdeki cekete daha **dikkatle** baktığımda onun benimki olmadığını **fark ettim.**

— Bana **başkasının** ceketini getirmişsiniz. **Benimkine** çok **benziyor** ama benimkinin **arkasında** ufak bir **leke** vardı, bunda yok. **İçeride** buna benzer **başka** bir ceket var mı? diye sordum.

Birlikte odaya girdik. İçeride **bir sürü** ceket vardı, sırayla **hepsine** baktık ama **hiçbiri** benimki değildi.

— **Sanırım** bir başkası sizin ceketinizi **almış** ve size de kendisininkini **bırakmış. Bu tarz şeyler** bazen oluyor.

— Ceket **umurumda değil** ama bu kutuyu **ne yapacağız?**

— Kutuyu **açın**, içine **bakalım**, dedi garson.

Kutunun içinde **altın** bir **yüzük** vardı. Oldukça **pahalı** görünüyordu.

— Kutuyu **karakola** götürmeliyim. Kutunun **sahibi** belki buraya **gelmeyebilir** ama böyle değerli bir yüzüğü **kaybettiyse** onu aramak için **mutlaka** karakola gider.

Lokantadan **ayrılıp** polis karakoluna **gittim. Polis memurlarından** birine yüzüğü **göstererek:**

— **Birisi** yüzük **kaybetti** mi? diye sordum.

— Evet, bu sabah **genç bir adam** geldi. Trende **kaybettiği** yüzüğünü arıyordu.

— **Ama** ben bu yüzüğü **trende** değil lokantada **buldum**, dedim şaşırarak.

— Elinizdeki yüzük **o adamın** tarif ettiği yüzüğe çok **benziyor**. Adama **ulaşıp** karakola **gelmesini** söyleyeceğim. Burada **bekleyin** lütfen, diye yanıtladı memur.

Genç adamın karakola gelmesi **uzun sürmedi.** Polis ona yüzüğü **gösterirken** bir yandan da **parmağıyla** beni **işaret etti.** Genç adam bana **döndü.**

— Size çok **teşekkür ederim.** Bu yüzüğe **çok para verdim** ve trende kaybetmiştim.

— Ama ben onu trende **bulmadım.** Trene **binmedim** bile, dedim.

— **Nerede** buldunuz peki? diye sordu.

Ona tüm **hikayeyi** anlattım. Genç adam şaşkınlıkla:

— Siz trene binmediniz, ben de lokantaya gitmedim. Peki, **yüzüğüm** o ceketin içine **nasıl girdi**? diye sordu.

Konuşmamızı **dinleyen** polis memuru, adama **sorular** sormaya başladı.

— Trende **yanınızda** biri var mıydı?

— **Evet** ama **yüzünü** hatırlamıyorum.

— Ceketini **hatırlayabilirsiniz** belki. Bunun **gibi miydi**? diye sorarak genç adama benim ceketimi gösterdi.

— Evet, **buydu**! dedi genç heyecanla.

Ben, hırsızlıkla **suçlanacağımı** düşünerek **gerilmiştim**. Polis ise gülüyordu.

— Trende yanınızdaki **adam** sizin yüzüğünüzü **çaldı** ve lokantaya girdi. Lokantadan **ayrılırken** doğru ceketi **almadı**. **Yakalanmak** istemediği için de lokantaya **geri dönmekten** korktu. **Hırsızlar,** her zaman korkarlar.

Genç adam **yüzüme** baktı.

— **Özür dilerim**. Ben yüzüğümü buldum ama siz ceketinizi **kaybettiniz.**

— Hiç **önemli değil**, zaten **eskiydi**, dedim gülümseyerek.

Hikayenin Özeti

Anlatıcı, iş seyahatlerinden birindedir. Her zaman yaptığı gibi bir şeyler yemek için bir lokantaya girer. Yemeği bitirdikten sonra garsondan ceketini getirmesini ister. Anlatıcı, ceketi ondan alırken yere bir şey düşer. İçinde bir yüzük olan anlatıcıya ait olmayan bir kutudur bu. Cekete daha dikkatli baktığında onun başka birinin ceketi olduğunu fark eder.

Anlatıcı, kime ait olduğunu bulmak için yüzüğü ve ceketi polis karakoluna götürür. Yüzük, genç bir adama aittir fakat adam lokantaya hiç gitmemiştir. Sonunda polis, olanların sırrını açıklar.

Summary of the story

The narrator is on one of his business trips. As he always does, he goes into a restaurant to have something to eat. After he has finished the meal, he asks waiter to bring his jacket. As the narrator takes his jacket from him, something falls out on the floor. It is a box with a ring inside, which doesn't belong to the narrator. When he looks at the jacket more carefully, he realizes that it's someone else's jacket.

The narrator takes the ring and jacket to the police station to find out whose ring it is. It belongs to a young man but he has never been in the restaurant. Finally, the police reveals the secret of what happened.

Vocabulary

- **aşağı yukarı:** more or less
- **işim:** my work
- **vardığımda:** when I arrived
- **lokantaya:** to restaurant (dative)
- **genellikle:** usually
- **aynı:** same
- **tanıyorlardı:** they knew
- **ceketimi:** my jacket (accusative)
- **götürdü:** he took
- **müşterilerin:** customers' (possessive)
- **askıya:** hanger (dative)
- **yedim:** I ate
- **beni:** me (accusative)
- **muhabbet ettim:** I chatted
- **hazırdım:** I was ready
- **getirmesini:** him to bring (accusative)
- **garson:** waiter
- **giyecek:** [you] will put
- **taşıyacaksınız:** you will carry
- **bugün:** today
- **elimde:** in my hand (locative)
- **yanıtladım:** I replied

- **aldığım sırada:** as I took
- **düştü:** it fell
- **eğilip:** bending down (adverb)
- **aldı:** he took
- **verdi:** he gave
- **buyrun:** here (imperative, plural/formal)
- **küçük:** little
- **kutu:** box
- **bakarak:** looking at (adverb)
- **bu ne:** what's this
- **benim değil:** it's not mine
- **görmedim:** I did not see
- **sizin:** your (plural/formal)
- **düştüğünü:** that it fell (accusative)
- **haklıydı:** he was right
- **yanlış:** wrong
- **dikkatle:** carefully
- **fark ettim:** I realized
- **başkasının:** someone else's
- **benimkine:** mine (dative)
- **benziyor:** looks like
- **arkasında:** back of (locative)
- **leke:** stain

- **içeride:** inside (locative)
- **başka:** another
- **birlikte:** together
- **bir sürü:** a lot of
- **hepsine:** all of them (dative)
- **hiçbiri:** none
- **sanırım:** I guess
- **almış:** he/she has taken
- **bırakmış:** he/she has left
- **bu tarz şeyler:** this kind of things
- **umurumda değil:** I don't care
- **ne yapacağız:** what we are going to do
- **açın:** open (imperative, plural/formal)
- **bakalım:** let's look (optative)
- **altın:** gold
- **yüzük:** ring
- **pahalı:** expensive
- **karakola:** to police station (dative)
- **sahibi:** its owner
- **gelmeyebilir:** he may not come
- **kaybettiyse:** if he has lost
- **mutlaka:** definitely
- **ayrılıp:** leaving (adverb)

- **gittim:** I went
- **polis memurları:** policemen
- **göstererek:** showing (adverb)
- **birisi:** someone
- **kaybetti:** he/she has lost
- **genç bir adam:** a young man
- **kaybettiği:** that he lost
- **ama:** but
- **trende:** in train (locative)
- **buldum:** I found
- **adamın:** that man's
- **benziyor:** it looks
- **ulaşıp:** reaching (adverb)
- **gelmesini:** him to come (accusative)
- **bekleyin:** wait (imperative, plural/formal)
- **uzun sürmedi:** it didn't take long
- **gösterirken:** while showing
- **parmağıyla:** with his finger
- **işaret etti:** he pointed
- **döndü:** he turned
- **teşekkür ederim:** thank you (interjection)
- **çok para verdim:** I paid a lot
- **bulmadım:** I didn't find

- **binmedim:** I didn't get on
- **nerede:** where (locative)
- **hikayeyi:** the story (accusative)
- **yüzüğüm:** my ring
- **nasıl:** how
- **girdi:** it got in
- **dinleyen:** listening (adjective)
- **sorular:** questions
- **yanınızda:** next to you (locative)
- **evet:** yes (interjection)
- **yüzünü:** his face (accusative)
- **hatırlayabilirsiniz:** you may remember
- **gibi miydi:** was it like
- **buydu:** this was it

- **suçlanacağımı:** that I would be accused of (accusative)
- **gerilmiştim:** I was nervous
- **adam:** the man
- **çaldı:** he stole
- **ayrılırken:** when leaving
- **almadı:** he didn't take
- **yakalanmak:** to get caught (infinitive)
- **geri dönmekten:** to go back (ablative)
- **hırsızlar:** thieves
- **yüzüme:** my face (dative)
- **özür dilerim:** I apologize (interjection)
- **kaybettiniz:** you've lost (plural/formal)
- **önemli değil:** it doesn't matter
- **eskiydi:** it was old

Questions about the story

1. **Anlatıcı, ceketini nerede kaybetti?**

   a) Trende.
   b) Barda.
   c) Lokantada.
   d) Takside.

2. **Anlatıcı, yüzüğü bulduğunda ...**

   a) Karakola götürdü.
   b) Kuyumcuya götürdü.
   c) Hanımına verdi.
   d) Lokantada bıraktı.

3. **Genç adam, yüzüğü ... kaybetmişti.**

   a) Lokantada.
   b) Takside.
   c) Metroda.
   d) Trende.

4. **Onlar hırsızı yakalayabildiler. Doğru mu, yanlış mı?**

   a) Doğru.
   b) Yanlış.

5. **Anlatıcı, lokantadaki ceketin ona ait olmadığını nasıl fark etti?**

   a) Garson söyledi.
   b) Cebinde yırtık vardı.
   c) Rengi farklıydı.
   d) Kendi ceketinden daha temizdi.

Answers

1) C – In the restaurant.
2) A – He took it to the police station.
3) D – In the train.
4) B – False.
5) D – It was more clear than his jacket.

CONCLUSİON

We hope you've enjoyed our stories and the way we've presented them. Each chapter, as you will have noticed, was a way to practice a language tool that you will regularly use when speaking Turkish.

Never forget: learning a language doesn't *have* to be a boring activity if you find the proper way to do it. Hopefully, we've provided you with a hands-on, fun way to expand your knowledge in Turkish, and you can apply your lessons to future ventures.

Feel free to use this book further ahead when you need to go back to remembering vocabulary and expressions — in fact, we encourage it.

Believe in yourself and never be ashamed of making mistakes. Even the best can fall; it's those who get up who can achieve greatness! Take care!

P.S. Keep an eye out for more books like this one; we're not done teaching you Turkish! Head over to www.LingoMastery.com and read our articles and sign up for our newsletter. We give away so much free stuff that will accelerate your Turkish learning, and you don't want to miss that!

MORE BOOKS BY LINGO MASTERY

Have you been trying to learn Turkish and simply can't find the way to expand your vocabulary?

Do your teachers recommend you boring textbooks and complicated stories that you don't really understand?

Are you looking for a way to learn the language quicker without taking shortcuts?

If you answered *"Yes!"* to at least one of those previous questions, then this book is for you! We've compiled the **2000 Most Common Words in Turkish,** a list of terms that will expand your vocabulary to levels previously unseen.

Did you know that — according to an important study — learning the top two thousand (2000) most frequently used words will enable you to understand up to **84%** of all non-fiction and **86.1%** of fiction literature and **92.7%** of oral speech? Those are *amazing* stats, and this book will take you even further than those numbers!

In this book:

A detailed introduction with tips and tricks on how to improve your learning

A list of **2000** of the most common words in Turkish and their translations

An example sentence for each word – in both Turkish *and* English

Finally, a conclusion to make sure you've learned and supply you with a final list of tips

Don't look any further, we've got what you need right here!

In fact, we're ready to turn you into a Turkish speaker... are you ready to become one?

Made in the USA
Las Vegas, NV
30 October 2023

79993077R00108